Mornings with Thérèse of Lisieux

compiled by Patricia Treece

CHARIS

SERVANT PUBLICATIONS
ANN ARBOR, MICHIGAN

Charis Books is an imprint of Servant Publications especially designed to serve Roman Catholics.

All scripture quotes marked RSV are from the Revised Standard Version of the Bible, © 1946, 1952, 1971 by the Division of Christian Education of the National Council of Churches of Christ in the USA. Used by permission. All other scripture quotes are St. Thérèse's paraphrases translated from the original French.

From *The Autobiography of St. Thérèse of Lisieux*, translated by John Beevers. Translation © 1957 by Doubleday, a division of Bantam Doubleday Dell Publishing Group, Inc. Used by permission.

From *General Correspondence I*. Translated by John Clarke, O.C.D. © 1982 Washington Province of Discalced Carmelite Friars, Inc. 1982, ICS Publications, 2131 Lincoln Road, N.E., Washington, D.C. 20002 U.S.A.

From *General Correspondence II*. Translated by John Clarke, O.C.D. © 1982 Washington Province of Discalced Carmelite Friars, Inc. 1988, ICS Publications, 2131 Lincoln Road, N.E., Washington, D.C. 20002 U.S.A.

While every effort has been made to trace copyright holders, if there should be any error or omission, the publishers will be happy to rectify this at the first opportunity.

Published by Servant Publications
P.O. Box 8617
Ann Arbor, Michigan 48107

Cover design: Left Coast Design, Inc., Portland, OR
Photographs: Central Photo Office of Lisieux. All rights reserved.

02 03 04 05 11 10 9 8 7 6

Printed in the United States of America
ISBN 1-56955-059-X

LIBRARY OF CONGRESS CATALOGING-IN-PUBLICATION DATA

Thérèse, de Lisieux, Saint, 1873-1897.
[Selections. Endligh. 1997]
Mornings with Thérèse of Lisieux / compiled by Patricia Treece.
    p.   cm.
Includes bibliographical references.
ISBN 1-56955-059-X
1. Catholic Church—Prayer-books and devotions—English.   I. Treece, Patricia.   II. Title.
BX2179.T49E5   1997
282'.092—dc21   97-20512 CIP

Mornings with
Thérèse of Lisieux

This book is for Therese, my sister and friend,

and for

great-hearted John Butler

The Family

Father
Louis Martin

Mother
Zélie Guerin Martin

Children
Marie (February 1860-January 1940)
Pauline(September 1862-July 1951)
Léonie (June 1863-June 1941)
Hélène (October 1864-February 1870,)
Joseph Louis (September 1866-February 1867)
Joseph Jean Baptist (December 1867-August 1868)
Céline (April 1869-February 1959)
Melanie Thérèse (August 1870-October 1870)
Francoise Thérèse (January 1873- September 1897)

Uncle
Isidore Guerin

Aunt
Céline Guerin

Cousins
Jeanne and Marie

Prioress of Carmel: Mother Marie de Gonzague

Missionaries who become Thérèse's adopted brothers after her

Prioress asks her to support their apostolic work with prayer.

Abbé Maurice Belliere
Père Adolphe Roulland

Introduction

"Mystic, comic, everything! She can make you weep with devotion and just as easily split your sides with laughter." So wrote Sister Marie of the Angels, novice mistress at the Lisieux Carmelite cloister in 1893, describing the buoyant, twenty-year-old Thérèse Martin. Thérèse had come to the Carmel at age fifteen, with "a head full of mischief" and a burning zeal to please God. More than once her clumsiness earned her a rebuke from her superiors about how she swept the cloister. But one day, Pope Pius X would call this pure, simple girl "the greatest saint of modern times." As her novice mistress then noted, Thérèse had "hiding within her a wisdom, a perfection." It would, in time, mark her for sainthood.

A century has passed since the twenty-four-year-old nun died in the remote Normandy cloister, virtually unknown. But since that day she has been credited with hundreds of astounding works for God—bringing cures to the dying, rescuing men on battlefields, appearing in mission lands where conversions have increased dramatically. Today, millions love St. Thérèse of Lisieux, not only for her wisdom, but for her unwavering passion to serve God, both in life and in death.

How did so brief a life yield such a prodigious legacy? St. Thérèse's story of love and self-sacrifice has its beginnings in memorable childhood, as the treasured youngest sister in a large and loving Norman family.

"My earliest recollections are of tender caresses and smiles," she wrote. "I was always cherished with the most loving care.… " She was the ninth child of Louis and Zélie Martin, extraordinarily gifted parents "more worthy of heaven than of earth," as Thérèse put it, because they loved God, each other, and their children at the very heights of charity. Thérèse's birth was awaited eagerly by her mother, who had lost four children before her to death when they were infants or toddlers. "I was born to be a mother!" Zélie once wrote.

Thérèse also experienced the cherishing of a "foster" mother, Rose Taille, who saved the baby with the milk of her breasts for fifteen months when her own mother could not feed her. Rose nourished the baby with smiles and love, trundling her in a hay-filled wheelbarrow into the fields and tying Thérèse "on to the back of a placid cow" at milking time.

When Thérèse was four-and-a-half, Zélie died of breast cancer. The second-oldest of her five daughters, sixteen-year-old Pauline, took over the mothering of Thérèse as seventeen-year-old Marie occupied herself with eight-year-old Céline. Pauline nurtured Thérèse, who affectionately would call her big sister "little mother." Thérèse would always have an intimate, loving relationship with Pauline, who "sowed joy all her life," and proved worthy of Zélie's dying words to her, "I know you'll become a nun and a saint."

When Pauline entered the Lisieux Carmelite cloister, Thérèse's godmother, Marie, a generous-hearted young woman, took over mothering Thérèse. Marie cared for Thérèse for the rest of her childhood, until she, too, became a Carmelite. Thérèse later wrote that she knew all about "the depths of tenderness in more than one mother's heart." And not only had she known four outstanding mothers, she had a saintly, loving aunt-by-marriage, Céline Guerin, who participated so closely in Thérèse's upbringing that Thérèse, in later letters, frequently called herself Céline's "daughter."

Thérèse also had a tender relationship with her father. Like Zélie, Louis firmly demanded good behavior, but gave his five daughters plenty of love and attention. At sixteen, Thérèse wrote to Louis, "The longer I live, my dearest Father, the more I love you.... When I think of you, I naturally think of God, for I cannot believe it possible to find anyone holier than you." Thérèse's assessment of her father was accurate. Both of her parents, as well as her sister Leonie, are candidates for beatification.

Thérèse's early environment was so drenched in wholesome spirituality that she could readily grasp God as Love, Truth, and Mercy. Her upbringing made Thérèse Martin a person who loved generously, rejoiced in intimacy, practiced great self-discipline, and was capable of honesty and humor about herself and others.

Her response to the things of God went higher and deeper than that of most souls. Even as a child she was concerned over the apparent injustice that some in heaven have more glory than others. Pauline comforted her by filling a small and a large glass. "See, they both have all they can hold."

In spite of her many advantages, Thérèse began to know suffering at an early age. Zélie's death caused her youngest child's ebullient personality to wither into timidity and over-sensitiveness for years. Pauline's departure for Carmel weakened Thérèse's immune system and opened the door to a sort of breakdown and mysterious illness: the ten-year-old almost died until a vision of Mary cured her instantaneously. When Thérèse herself entered Carmel at the age of fifteen, she suffered having to leave Louis and her sister closest in age, Céline, whom she called "the sweet echo of my soul."

Later, when Céline told her father that she too—the last of his five daughters at home—wished to enter the cloister, he acquiesced, but, his daughters later believed, his sense of loss may have played a part in a series of strokes which affected him mentally. In his confusion, he began running away and, one day, waved a gun, thinking he needed to protect his family. Thérèse was aware that criticism was being directed at the Martin girls for "abandoning their father." She also suffered deeply for his "humiliation" when Louis was confined to an insane asylum until he became docile enough to safely return to home care.

Other sources of anxiety were Léonie, the family's "problem child," who three times tried to become a nun and failed, and Céline, who, while putting off entering into Carmel in order to care for their father, attracted admirers that Thérèse feared might jeopardize her vocation.

Less visible were Thérèse's interior struggles to follow Jesus, with whom she had her most important relationship. Even a loving person like Thérèse has plenty of ego that must die to make room for God.

Thérèse studied the gospels ceaselessly. She loved them so much she wore a portion against her heart at all times.* She concluded that, to love as Christ called her to, she had to give up ownership of not just her time, talent, and the direction of her life, but small things, such as paintbrushes, her ideas, and even certain witticisms. To follow Christ, she felt she must not complain about being given old, dried-up food that was often her reward for not complaining no matter what she was served. She had to "not rush" to get a place by the fire at recreation, even though, being intensely sensitive to cold, she was frozen through. She would eventually contract the tuberculosis which killed her.

And to answer God's call to put Him first and love all *in* Him, she had to live in the same cloister with her beloved sisters, Marie, Pauline, and later Céline, maintaining the bonds of love, yet not the ease and the ardor of those bonds. That would defeat the purpose of becoming a contemplative nun. To love as Jesus loves, she often avoided her sisters, and instead, willingly put herself at the service of those unlovable nuns everyone else avoided. She did this so successfully that a nun, who irritated Thérèse almost beyond bearing, asked her sincerely, "Sister Thérèse, why are you so attracted to me?", and her sister Marie reproached her for seeming to care more for this nun than for Marie. Marie understood only later why Thérèse offered her no explanation, and responded only with a hearty laugh.

---

* She sewed a little bag with a string to go round her neck and in it kept the pages of one of the four gospels.

Given spiritual charge of a group of novices, Thérèse made certain not to dominate them with her own personality. Instead she approached them from "above the human level," relying totally on much prayer and truthfulness regarding their souls. She was equally willing to calmly "play the heavy" or to abase herself, whichever would benefit the novice in question. In these many ways Thérèse swept her soul clean of ego, that God might be her all in all and Christ, not Thérèse, might live and reign in her.

This difficult path to sanctity she humbly called her "little way of spiritual childhood." Based on what she had learned from Zélie, Rose, Louis, and her sisters, she knew she was serving a tender, loving God, who longs for our happiness, and who, far from punishing us for our faults, weaknesses, or even sins, clasps even the most prodigal of us to His heart as soon as we turn to Him regretting whatever we have done. Thérèse believed that the way to God's heart is to "gather flowers of love and sacrifice" by doing small, ego-killing good deeds for love of Him, not trusting in our spiritual accomplishments, but like a child, living with complete confidence in Him to provide, through His Son's infinite merits, the graces and virtues we need to gain heaven.

By the age of twenty-four, as she lay dying, Thérèse could laugh in perfect humility to her sisters, and say, "You know you're taking care of a little saint," crediting her sanctity to "[Him] who is mighty, who has done great things for me." Her intense desire, which she believed God would not leave unfulfilled, was not simply to become a saint, but to go to "the homeland," as she called

Heaven, and go on working till the end of time "to make God loved by a multitude of souls."

That Thérèse is a contemporary of our generation may be hard to imagine, but if her life span had matched that of two of her natural sisters, she would have died in the 1960s. Her autobiography, *The Story of a Soul* (pieced together from a memoir written at Pauline's request, a second memoir asked for by Prioress Marie de Gonzague, and a letter requested by Marie), has appeared in almost every language and has sold millions of copies. Her story made such an impact and generated so much interest, that, in the first twenty-eight years following her death, the twenty nuns at Thérèse's Lisieux Carmelite cloister sent out thirty million pictures of her in answer to requests from all over the world. Thirty years after her death, the pope named her co-patron saint of the missions and missionaries. Having promised, "I will come down," referring to the work she would do on earth after her death, Thérèse was seen repeatedly in mission lands, where annual conversions increased astoundingly from the year she died. The book *Messengers: After-Death Appearances of Saints and Mystics,* written (by this author) after work in the Lisieux Carmel archives, contains references to or complete details of nearly a hundred of Thérèse's visits to the world to do the work of God. They are only a sampling.

In her life and in her death, God has used Thérèse's wisdom to open many souls to Him. Much of that wisdom is contained in these pages. As you read this book, may Thérèse draw you closer to His love and light!

One Day, A Glorious Reward

—Early in 1870, Zélie Martin receives a letter from her only sister, a Visitation nun. Zélie's exceptional five-year-old has just died after a sudden illness. This is the third child to die of the seven Zélie has borne. Having longed to give the Church a missionary priest, she had rejoiced at the birth of two boys but each died before his first birthday. In spite of her intense grief, she accepts the three deaths as permitted for some reason that God will reveal to her in heaven if not here.

That faith and confidence of yours which never wavers will one day have their reward—a glorious one. Be quite sure that God will bless you and that the depths of your sufferings will be matched by the consolation reserved for you. For won't you be well recompensed if God, well pleased with you, gives you that great saint which, for His Glory, you have desired so greatly?

That fall Zélie bears another daughter, who lives only two months. Now in her forties, she feels there will be no more additions to the four daughters she has left. To her surprise she becomes pregnant again in 1872. Her ninth and last child—another girl—arrives January 2, 1873. Years later popes will speak not of a son of Zélie's but of this girl, Thérèse, as one of the Church's greatest missionaries ever and dub her "the greatest saint of modern times."

The Paper Cutter

—From May 14, 1876 letter from Thérèse's mother to second-oldest daughter, Pauline, at boarding school

2

Céline seems naturally good. As for the little minx*
[three-year-old Thérèse] I do not know how she will turn
out; she is such a little madcap, so thoughtless—[with] an intelligence superior to Céline's, but she is less gentle and has in her an almost invincible stubbornness; when she says "no," nothing can make her give in.

However she has a heart of gold, she is very affectionate and very honest; it is funny to see her running after me to [confess], "Mamma, I pushed Céline once, I struck her once, but I will not do it anymore." (It is like this for everything she does.)

At this moment [she's] very much taken up with cutting papers. Fortunately, she has the good habit of coming to show them to me to be sure she can cut them up. She is well-settled now in her little chair, cutting [and] singing with all her heart.

(Written later) Thérèse is in great grief. She broke a little vase and rushed to show it to me; I appeared somewhat displeased, and [she] was sad. A moment afterwards, she ran to me, saying: "Do not be sad, little Mother, when I earn some money, I assure you I will buy you another one."

---

* Clarke translates "ferret." As this has a negative connotation Zélie did not mean, I have substituted "minx."

"Mama, I Was Naughty."

—From February 13, 1877 letter from Thérèse's mother to Pauline

Little Thérèse [just turned four], whom we took [to the sermon] was really bored. She said: "It was more beautiful than usual, but it bores me just the same."

One morning I wanted to kiss her before going downstairs; she seemed to be in a deep sleep but Marie said, "Mamma, she is pretending." Then I bent over her forehead to kiss her, but she hid immediately under her blanket, saying with the air of a spoiled child, "I don't want anyone to see me." I was less than pleased and I made her feel it.

Two minutes later, I heard her crying and soon to my great surprise I saw her at my side. She had left her little bed all by herself, had come down the stairs barefooted, hampered by her nightgown which was longer than herself. Her little face was bathed in tears: "Mamma," she said, throwing herself at my knees, "Mamma, I was naughty, pardon me." Pardon was quickly granted. I took my cherub in my arms, pressing her to my heart and covering her with kisses.

Soap Bubbles and Cloisters

—*From April 4, 1877 letter by Pauline*

4

Thérèse [age 4] and Céline are in the garden, enjoying themselves blowing soap bubbles.

Tell [Sister] that in a few years she'll have a new novice: Thérèse Martin.

Yesterday evening, [Thérèse] said: "I'll be a religious in a cloister because Céline wants to. I must learn how to read to children, don't you see? But I won't conduct class because this would bore me too much. Céline will do it. I'll be Mother [Superior]. I'll walk all day in the cloister, and then I'll go with Céline; we'll play with our dolls."

"Dear Thérèse, do you know, you will have to keep silent?"

"Ah! What a pity! [but] I will say nothing."

"What will you do then?"

"That's no problem; I'll pray to good Jesus. But how will I pray to Him without saying anything? And who will show me since I'll be Mother? Tell me!"

I had a frightful desire to laugh [but] remained serious [because] she was speaking from her heart. Finally, after reflecting a few moments, she fixed her big blue eyes on me, and smiling mischievously, she gesticulated with her little arms like an adult, saying: "After all, *mon petit Paulin*, it's not worth tormenting myself. When I'm big like you and Marie, I'll be told what to do."

"That's it, dear baby," I answered, covering her with kisses.

Open Spaces

—Thérèse writes of her fourth year

How happy I was at that age. I was beginning to enjoy life and I felt the attraction of goodness. I think my character was the same then as now, for I already had very great self-control. How quickly they went, those golden days of my early childhood; yet what lovely memories I have of them. I remember so happily the days we went with Daddy to the Pavilion.* I can't forget the slightest detail. I remember above all the walks on Sunday when Mummy always came with us. I can still feel the deep emotion I felt when I saw the fields of wheat starred with poppies, cornflowers, and daisies. I was already in love with far distances, with open spaces, and with great trees.

---

* A six-sided tower with a garden, this was Louis Martin's refuge, purchased during his bachelor days in Alencon. There he kept his fishing gear, did some gardening and liked to be alone to meditate.

Dreams of Heaven

—Thérèse writes of being four and a half

The moment Mummy died (August 28, 1877) my happy disposition changed completely. I had been lively and cheerful, but I became timid and quiet and a bundle of nerves. A glance was often enough to make me burst into tears. I was only happy if no one took any notice of me, and I couldn't endure being with strangers. I was never cheerful except within the family circle [where] the greatest love and kindness surrounded me. Daddy's affection seemed enriched by a real motherly love, and I felt that both Pauline and Marie [her oldest sisters] were the most tender and self-sacrificing of mothers.

Every morning you [Pauline] came to me and I said my prayers kneeling at your side. Afterwards I had a reading lesson. "Heaven" was the first word I could read.

I particularly loved the days when my "beloved king"* took me with him when he went fishing, for I loved the countryside and its birds and flowers. I preferred to sit alone on the grass amid the flowers. Then I used to think very deeply, and though I knew nothing of meditation, my soul entered into a true state of prayer. Earth seemed a place of exile and I dreamed of heaven. I realized that only in heaven would I know unclouded joy.

* her father

First School Days

7

I was eight and a half [when she left lessons with Pauline to attend the local Benedictine abbey school as a day pupil]. I was more advanced than any child of my age, and I was put in a class of older pupils. One of them was between fourteen and fifteen. She wasn't at all intelligent, but she knew how to dominate the other pupils and even the mistresses. Though I was so young, I was nearly always at the top of the class and the nuns were very fond of me. So, very understandably, this girl was jealous of me and she [made me pay] in a thousand ways for my small triumphs. I was so timid and easily upset that I didn't know how to look out for myself. All I did was cry and say nothing. I didn't tell [anyone]. I was not strong enough to rise above it all, and so I suffered terribly. Fortunately I went home every evening. There I cheered up, jumped on Daddy's knee, told him the marks I'd been given, and a kiss from him made me forget all my troubles.

My Kind of Love

I tried to make friends with the girls at school who were of my own age, particularly with two of them. I really loved them and they loved me as far as they were capable of true love. But how small and feeble the human heart is! It wasn't long before I saw that they just didn't understand my kind of love. One of these girls had to go and stay with her family for some months. I thought about her all the time she was away and cherished a little ring she had given me. I was overjoyed when she came back, but she was quite cool towards me. She didn't understand how I loved her. I was upset, but didn't beg for an unwilling affection. Yet God has made me so that when once I love I love forever, and so I continue to pray for this girl and I love her still.

A Maid Remembers

—Thérèse's aunt's maid, Marcelline-Anne Huse—later a Benedictine nun—often cared for Thérèse with her cousins, Jeanne and Marie, and walked the three girls to the Benedictine school. Marcelline-Anne testified:

When Thérèse found herself alone with me on the walk [to school] or in the house, she behaved with great affection and assurance as she [shared with] me her little confidences. These intimate conversations just naturally tended to be on pious things. She was, for her age, exceptionally intelligent and reflective. I remember in particular how, even before she made her First Communion, when she heard some workers blaspheme, she explained to me, in order to excuse them, that one mustn't judge the depths of another soul—that these men had received far fewer graces than us and they were more miserable than guilty. She was very joyous and expansive in her family or with us. One could see that then she threw off the constraints she had to impose on herself at school. She esteemed the Benedictine sisters, her teachers, greatly; but she was ill at ease around her classmates because they were not interested, as were the members of her family, in the outpourings of her soul. But we only suspected her sufferings [at the school] because she never accused anyone and never complained.

A Kiss of Love

—On her First Communion (May 8, 1884)

Oh how sweet the first kiss of Jesus was. It was a kiss of love. I knew that I was loved and I declared: "I love You and I give myself to You forever." Jesus made no demand on me; He asked for no sacrifices. For a long time Jesus and little Thérèse had known and understood one another. That day our meeting was more than simple recognizing each other. It was perfect union. We were no longer two. Thérèse had disappeared like a drop of water lost in the immensity of the ocean; Jesus alone remained.

10

On Being Herself

My cousin Marie, who never had really good health, spent a lot of her time crying and complaining. My aunt used to soothe her and talk tenderly to her, but Marie would continue to cry and say how her head ached. I also had a headache nearly every day, but I hadn't complained. Now I decided to imitate Marie and began to cry. Like Marie, I said: "I've a headache." But I just could not make [her aunt and oldest cousin] believe that I cried because of a headache. Instead of fussing over me, they spoke to me as if I were a grown-up and reproached me for not being frank. So I was taught my lesson and made up my mind never to imitate anyone else.

"One of the Greatest Graces of My Life"

When I read stories [in late childhood] about the deeds of the great French heroines—especially of the Venerable Joan of Arc, I longed to imitate them and felt stirred by the same inspiration which moved them. It was then that I received one of the greatest graces of my life, for, at that age, I didn't receive the spiritual enlightenment which now floods my soul. I was made to understand that the glory I was to win would never be seen during my lifetime. My glory would consist in becoming a great saint! This desire might seem presumptuous, seeing how weak and imperfect I was and still am, even after eight years as a nun; yet I always feel the same fearless certainty that I shall become a great saint. I'm not relying on my own merits, as I have none, but I put my hope in Him who is goodness and holiness Himself. It is He alone who, satisfied with my feeble efforts, will raise me to Him, will clothe me with His infinite merits, and will make me a saint.

A Thrill of Pleasure

13

I left school when I was thirteen [in 1886] and had private lessons several times a week with Madame Papineau. She was a very good and well-educated woman who lived with her mother. Quite apart from what I learned, these lessons were useful because they made me know the world—which sounds surprising, I know. Sitting in that room full of old-fashioned furniture, I saw all kinds of visitors—priests, ladies, young girls, and others. Madame Papineau's mother used to do most of the talking so as to leave her daughter free to go on teaching me, but I didn't learn much when visitors were there. For though I kept my nose in my book, I heard all that was said, though it might have been better if I hadn't. One woman would say what lovely hair I had and another, thinking I couldn't hear her, would ask as she went toward the door, who was the young girl who was so pretty. These remarks, which were all the more flattering [because] I was not supposed to hear them, gave me a thrill of pleasure that showed me clearly how full of self-love I was. I'm always ready to sympathize with the people who lose their souls! After all, it's so easy once you begin to stray along the primrose path of worldliness.

On Chattering About Spiritual Things

—When Thérèse was thirteen

I remained before the Blessed Sacrament until Daddy came to take me home. There I found my sole comfort: Jesus, my only friend. I could talk only to Him about religion. I felt it better to speak to God than about Him. There's often so much self-love involved in chatter about spiritual things!

Her Oversensitivity and Its Sudden Healing

15

I did not deserve the graces heaven showered on me. I had many faults. It's true that I longed to be good, but I had an odd way of going about it. As I was the youngest, I wasn't used to looking after myself. Céline tidied our bedroom and I never did a stroke of housework. But after Marie entered Carmel [October 15, 1886], I sometimes used to make our beds—to please God. Sometimes, too, when Céline was away, I looked after her plants. As I did this for no other reason than to please God, I shouldn't have expected any thanks for it. Yet if Céline didn't look surprised and pleased, I cried with disappointment.

My extreme sensitiveness made me quite unendurable. If I ever offended anyone accidentally, instead of making the best of it, I wept bitterly and so made things worse. Then, when I'd stopped weeping, I'd start all over again and weep for having wept. I couldn't cure myself. It needed God to perform a small miracle to make me grown-up in a second, and this miracle He performed on Christmas Day [1886]. [Jesus] flooded the darkness of my soul with torrents of light. My tears dried up. [I] got back for good the strength of soul lost when [I was] four and a half. Love filled my heart, I forgot myself, and henceforth I was happy.

Many Graces

16

—In Thérèse's fourteenth year

As the *Imitation* says, God sometimes reveals Himself "in great light" or "appears veiled under signs and figures," and it was in this [second] way that He disclosed Himself to us [Thérèse and her blood sister-soulmate Céline]. But how light and transparent was the veil which hid Jesus from our eyes! Doubt wasn't possible and faith and hope were no longer needed, for love made us find on earth Him we sought: "When we were alone He gave us His kiss, and now no one may despise us."

Such tremendous graces had to bear fruit and it was abundant. To be good became natural and pleasant for us. At first my face often betrayed the struggle I was having. But gradually spontaneous self-sacrifice came easily. Jesus said: "If ever a man is rich, gifts will be made to Him, and his riches will abound." For every grace I made good use of, He gave me many more.

Love Tokens

When I realized [at age fourteen] how trifling are the sacrifices of this life compared with the rewards of heaven, I wanted to love Jesus, to love Him passionately, and to give Him a thousand tokens of my love while I still could. *[At a later age she put a similar thought into poetry]:*

My life is but an instant, an hour that passes by,
A single day that slips my grasp and quickly
slides away.
O well you know, my dearest God, to love you,
I only have today!

On Holy Communion

18

Our Lord does not come down from Heaven every day to lie in a golden ciborium. He comes to find another heaven which is infinitely dearer to Him—the heaven of our souls.

"In Love One Says a Thousand Silly Things"

One evening, not knowing how to tell Jesus how much I loved Him and how much I longed for Him to be served and honored everywhere, I thought with sadness that not a single act of love ever ascended from the gulfs of hell. I cried that I would gladly be plunged into that realm of blasphemy and pain so that even there He could be loved forever. Of course that would not glorify Him, for all He wants is our happiness; yet when one's in love one says a thousand silly things.

A New, Intense Longing

20

One Sunday [in 1887] when I was looking at a picture of Our Lord on the Cross, I saw the Blood coming from one of His hands, and I felt terribly sad to think that It was falling to the earth and that no one was rushing forward to catch It. I determined to stay continually at the foot of the Cross and receive It. I knew that I should then have to spread It among other souls. The cry of Jesus on the Cross—"I am thirsty"—rang continually in my heart and set me burning with a new, intense longing. I wanted to quench the thirst of my Well-Beloved and I myself was consumed with a thirst for souls.

On Thérèse's Chastity

—Process testimony of her oldest sister, Marie

Regarding her trip to Rome [on an 1887 pilgrimage with Céline and their father], she wrote: "I begged Our Lady of Victory to keep away from me anything that might tarnish my purity. I was not ignorant that during a trip, like that to Italy, one could encounter many things capable of troubling me, above all because not knowing evil, I feared to discover it."

She was so pure and so simple at the same time, that one could confide in her every kind of temptation on the subject of purity. One felt that she would not be troubled by it.

21

"My Soul Soared"

On our way to Rome we crossed Switzerland and saw its mountains with their snow-covered summits lost in clouds, its waterfalls, its deep valleys thick with huge ferns and purple heather. It was wonderfully good for me to see all the richness of this natural loveliness. My soul soared up to Him who delights to scatter such masterpieces over the place where we spend our brief time of exile.

How can I describe what I felt before the wonder and poetry of these scenes? They were a foretaste of the splendors of heaven. I saw life in a convent as it really is, with all its restrictions and its little daily hidden sacrifices. I realized how easy it would be to become wrapped up in oneself and to forget the sublime purpose of our vocation. I said: "Later, in the hour of trial and when I am imprisoned in Carmel and able to see only a small patch of sky, I shall recall today and it will give me strength. All my trifling affairs will be lost in the power and majesty of God. I shall love only Him and I shall escape the misfortune of attaching myself to trifles, now that I have glimpsed what He has in store for those who love Him."

"That I Might Be a Martyr"

I can't possibly describe the emotion which set me trembling as I stood before the Coliseum, the arena where so many martyrs had shed their blood for Jesus. I longed to kiss the ground sanctified by their glorious combats. But how disappointed I was! A barrier prevented our getting to [the actual area]. No one dared to venture into the heart of those dangerous ruins. But to have come all the way to Rome without going down into the arena was impossible. I thought of one thing only—how to get into the arena.

[Stooping down, I saw] what I was looking for. With a cry of joy I shouted to Céline: "Come on! Follow me! We can get down!" We rushed off together, clambering over the ancient stonework which crumbled under our feet. Daddy, startled by our rashness, shouted after us.

[Céline] remembered [mention of] a small paving stone marked with a cross which was the place where the martyrs died. She soon found it. We knelt on the sacred spot and our souls joined in the same prayer. My heart beat fast as I pressed my lips to the dust reddened by the blood of the first Christians. I begged that I too might be a martyr for Jesus and I felt deep within me that my prayer was granted.

Of Mortifications

24

How did I spend those three months [before being permitted to enter the cloistered religious order of Carmel at age fifteen instead of having to wait to the more usual age of twenty-one]?

At first I thought I ought to relax and lead a less constricted life than usual, but God made me realize what benefit I could get from this time of waiting. I resolved to lead a life of greater devoutness and mortification than ever before. When I speak of mortification, I don't mean the kind of penance practiced by saints. There are great souls who practice every sort of mortification from childhood, but I am not like them. All I did was to break my self-will, check a hasty reply, and do little kindnesses without making a fuss about them—and lots of similar things. So I prepared myself to become the bride of Jesus.

"The Nearer One Gets to God"

The novice mistress was a true saint, a perfect model of the
first Carmelites. I spent most of my time with her, as it was
her job to teach me to work. Her kindness was beyond
words. I appreciated all she did for me and I loved her dearly.
Yet I could not be frank with her. I didn't know how to express
what was happening within me, for I was ignorant of the right
words for it. So my periods of direction were a torture, a real martyrdom.

One of the old nuns seemed to understand what I was going
through. At recreation one day she said: "It strikes me, my child,
that you cannot have much to say to your superiors."

"Why do you think that, Mother?"

"Because your soul is very simple. But when you are perfect, you
will be more simple still. The nearer one gets to God, the simpler
one becomes."

Without a Word

—During her trial period as a Carmelite

I tried hard not to make excuses. This was very difficult, especially where our novice mistress was concerned, for I wanted to hide nothing from her.

My first victory was not a big one, but it cost me a great deal. A small vase, which someone had left lying behind a window, was found broken. Our novice mistress thought I was guilty of leaving it lying about. She was cross, told me I was thoroughly untidy, and ordered me to be more careful in the future. Without a word, I kissed the ground and promised not to be untidy again. These trifles cost me a lot because I was so lacking in virtue. I had to remember that all would be revealed on the Day of Judgment.

Desertion: A Form of Courage

27

My last way of avoiding defeat in combat was desertion. I was already using this method during my novitiate and it always succeeded for me perfectly. Here's an example, Mother [Marie de Gonzague], that I think will make you smile:

One time when you had bronchitis, I came very quietly to return keys; this chance to see you made me very happy. A sister thought I was going to waken you and, out of holy zeal, tried to quietly take the keys from me. But I was too wicked to give up *my rights*. I told her as politely as possible, that I was as desirous as she to be quiet, adding it was my duty to return them. Nowadays I realize it would have been much better simply to give them to her but, then, I struggled to push my way into the room.

The noise woke you and all the blame fell on me! The poor sister made quite a speech, the gist of which was "Sister Thérèse did it!" I wanted to defend myself but knew without a doubt that if I opened my mouth I'd lose my soul's peace; I also knew I hadn't enough virtue to be accused and say nothing [so] I fled—heart beating so violently I had to plunk myself down on the stairs to enjoy the fruits of victory.

Sleeping Jesus

—On retreat in January, 1889, Thérèse writes to her fellow Carmelite and blood sister Pauline

[Jesus] is riddling me with *pinpricks:* the poor little ball [she liked to refer to herself as a toy for the Child Jesus to enjoy] is exhausted. All over it has very little holes which make it suffer more than if it had only one large one! Nothing near Jesus. Aridity! Sleep! But at least there is silence! Silence does good to the soul. But creatures! Oh! Creatures! The little ball shudders from them!

Those who surround me are very good, but there is something—I don't know what—that repels me! I cannot give you any explanation. I am, however, very *happy*—happy to suffer what Jesus wants me to suffer. If He doesn't directly puncture His little ball, it is really He who directs the hand that punctures it! [Thérèse refers to a particular nun she found very trying.] Since Jesus wants to sleep why will I hinder Him? I am only too happy that He doesn't bother with me, for He is showing me that I am not a stranger when treating me this way, for I assure you, He is going to no trouble about carrying on a conversation with me!

A Precious, Bitter Cross

—Regarding her father's strokes and dementia

January 10th [1889 when Thérèse was clothed in the Carmelite habit] was Father's day of triumph—[his] Palm Sunday. Like his Divine Master, his day of glory was followed by a grievous passion and, just as the sufferings of Jesus pierced the heart of His Mother, so our hearts were torn by the suffering and humiliation of the one we loved more than anyone on earth.

In June, 1888, I [had] astonished our novice mistress by saying: "I am suffering a lot [from his illness], but I feel I can endure much more." I didn't know then that a month after my Clothing Day our dear father would have to drink so bitter a cup [suffering dementia, he was confined to an insane asylum]. Then I didn't say I could suffer more! Words can't describe our agony, so I shan't try.

In heaven, we shall enjoy talking of these gloomy days, for the three years of father's martyrdom seem to me to have been the sweetest and most fruitful period of our lives. I would not exchange them for the most wonderful ecstasies. Sweet and precious this bitter cross was, since we felt nothing but love and gratitude for it. We no longer walked along the way of perfection—we flew.

[Suffering spiritual dryness], my longing to suffer was granted to the full, yet I was as happy as could be.

Running After Jesus

Since Jesus has gone to Heaven, I can follow Him only by the traces He has left. But how radiant and how fragrant these traces are! I have only to glance at the Holy Gospels and at once I breathe the fragrance of His life and know which way to run. I rush to the lowest place, not the highest, and repeat, with the greatest confidence, the humble prayer of the publican. Above all I imitate Mary Magdalene, for her amazing—or rather her loving—audacity which won the Heart of Jesus captivates mine.

On the Intercessory Prayers of Saints and Angels

31 I remembered the prayer of Eliseus to the prophet Elias, and so I stood before the angels and the assembly of saints and said: "I am the smallest of creatures and I recognize my worthlessness, but I also know how hearts that are generous and noble love to do good. So I beseech you, happy dwellers in heaven, to adopt me as your child. I implore you to obtain for me [through prayer] a double portion of your love of God!"

O Lord, I cannot fathom the full implication of my prayer. I know that if I could, I should be afraid of being crushed by its rashness. But my excuse is that I am a child and children don't think what their words mean.

What True Charity Consists Of

I began to consider just how Jesus had loved His disciples. I saw it was not for their natural qualities, for I recognized they were ignorant men and often preoccupied with earthly affairs. Yet He calls them His friends and His brethren. He wants to see them near Him in the kingdom of His Father and to open this kingdom to them He wills to die on the Cross. As I meditated I saw how imperfect was my love for the other nuns and I knew that I did not love them as Jesus loves them. But now I realize that true charity consists in putting up with all one's neighbor's faults, never being surprised by his weakness, and being inspired by the least of his virtues.

On Love

In Carmel, of course, one has no enemies, but one certainly has natural likes and dislikes. One feels attracted to a certain sister and one would go out of one's way to dodge meeting another. Jesus tells me that it is this very sister I must love, and I must pray for her even though her attitude makes me believe she has no love for me. "For if you love those who love you, what reward have you?" (RSV) Do not even sinners love those that love them? It is not enough to love. We must prove that we do. We naturally like to please a friend, but that is not charity, for so do sinners.

Every Artist Likes to Have His Works Praised

34

Formerly one of our nuns managed to irritate me whatever she did or said. Because I didn't want to give way to my natural dislike for her, I told myself charity was not a matter of feelings but of deeds. So I set myself to do for this sister exactly what I'd do for the one I loved most. Every time I met her I prayed for her, offering God all her virtues and her merits. I was sure this would please Jesus, for every artist likes to have his works praised.

Not contenting myself with praying a lot for this nun who caused me so much struggle, I tried to do as many things for her as I could, and whenever I was tempted to speak disagreeably to her, I contented myself with giving her my best smile and trying to change the subject.

When the struggle became too severe, I fled like a deserter. [Completely unaware of how I felt], she asked me one day very happily: "Sister Thérèse, please tell me, what attracts you so much to me?" Ah, what attracted me was Jesus hidden in the depth of her soul. Jesus, who makes the bitter sweet!

Sweating Out Charity

35

Being charitable has not always been so pleasant for me. [For instance] at meditation I was for a long time near a sister who never stopped fidgeting with either her rosary or something else. Perhaps I was the only one who heard her but how it irritated me. What I wanted to do was turn and stare at her until she stopped her noise, but deep down I knew it was better to endure it patiently—first, for the love of God and, secondly, so as not to upset her. So I made no fuss, though sometimes I was soaked with sweat under the strain and my prayer was nothing but the prayer of suffering. At last I tried to find some way of enduring this suffering calmly and even joyfully. So I did my best to enjoy this unpleasant little noise. Instead of trying not to hear it—which was impossible—I strove to listen to it carefully as if it were a first-class concert, and my meditation, *which was not the prayer of quiet*, was spent in offering this concert to Jesus.

Doing the Smallest Actions for Love

Great deeds are forbidden me. I cannot preach the Gospel nor shed my blood—but what does it matter? My brothers toil instead of me and I, a little child, keep close by the throne of God and I *love* for those who fight. Love proves itself by deeds. I will scatter flowers, perfuming the Divine Throne, and I'll sweetly sing my hymn of love. These flowers are every little sacrifice, every glance and word, and the doing of the least of actions for love.

36

Just As Dear

I was far from getting any consolation. Instead, I suffered complete spiritual dryness, almost as if I were quite forsaken. As usual, Jesus slept in my little boat. I know that other souls rarely let Him sleep peacefully, and He is so wearied by the advances He is always making that He hastens to take advantage of the rest I offer Him. It's likely that, as far as I'm concerned, He will stay asleep until the great final retreat of eternity. But that doesn't upset me. It fills me with great joy. It's true that I'm a long way from being a saint, and this attitude of mine proves it. Instead of delighting in my spiritual aridity, I ought to blame my lack of faith and fervor for it. I should be distressed that I drop off to sleep during my prayers and during my thanksgiving after Holy Communion. But I don't feel at all distressed. I know that children are just as dear to their parents whether they are asleep or awake and I know that doctors put their patients to sleep before they operate. So I just think that God "knows our frame; he remembers that we are dust" (RSV).

No Earthly Things

—Making her Carmelite vows in September 1890

I [was] in that "peace which surpasseth all understanding." I demanded innumerable favors. I felt that I was really a queen and I made full use of my title to ask the King for every kind of benefit for His ungrateful subjects. I forgot no one. I wanted every sinner to be converted that day and for purgatory to be emptied. Next to my heart I carried this letter saying what I wanted for myself: "O Jesus, let my baptismal robe remain forever white. Take me, rather than let me stain my soul by the slightest deliberate fault. Let me neither look for nor find anyone but You and You alone. Let all creatures be as nothing to me and me as nothing to them. Let no earthly things disturb my peace. O Jesus, I ask only for peace—peace and, above all, *love* that is without measure or limits. May I die as a martyr for You. Give me martyrdom of soul or body. Ah! rather give me both! Enable me to fulfill all my duties perfectly and let me be ignored, trodden underfoot, and forgotten like a grain of sand. To You, my Beloved, I offer myself so that You may fulfill in me Your holy will without a single creature placing any obstacle in the way."

At the close of that lovely day I thought that I should soon ascend to heaven and be united with my divine Spouse in eternal happiness.

Launched on the Tide of Confidence and Love

39 I usually find preached retreats most trying [but] God used [Father Prou*] to help me. I'd had all kinds of spiritual troubles then which I had felt incapable of talking about, but I suddenly found I could express myself. The priest was wonderfully understanding and divined what I was getting at. He launched me full sail on the tide of confidence and love which attracted me so much, but upon which I had not dared to venture. He told me my [unintended] faults did not distress God.

I was tremendously happy at hearing such consoling words. I'd never before heard it said that one's faults did not distress God, and I was overwhelmed with joy at this assurance. It gave me patience to endure this life of exile. It was, too, the echo of my own inmost thoughts. For a long time I had realized that Our Lord was more tender than a mother—and how well I know the depths of tenderness in more than one mother's heart! I know that a mother is always ready to forgive the unintentional misbehavior of her child. I've experienced that so many times myself: a single hug moved me far more than any reprimand. With my temperament, fear makes me shrink back, but love makes me come forward—or rather, I fly!

* A Franciscan who gave the Carmelites a retreat in 1891.

The Folly of Jesus' Love

O Eternal Word, my Savior, You are the Eagle I love and the one who fascinates me. You swept down to this land of exile and suffered and died so that You could bear away every soul and plunge them into the heart of the Blessed Trinity, that inextinguishable furnace of love. You re-entered the splendors of heaven, yet stayed in our vale of tears hidden under the appearance of a white Host so that You can feed me with Your own substance. O Jesus, do not be angry if I tell You that Your love is a mad love, and how can You expect my heart, when confronted with this folly, not to soar up to You? How can there be any limit to my trust?

After Communion

What can I tell you of my thanksgiving after Holy Communion? I have less consolation then than I ever have! And it's very natural, for I don't want Our Lord to visit me for my own satisfaction, but only for His pleasure.

I picture my soul as a patch of bare ground and I beg the Blessed Virgin to clear it of all rubbish (my imperfections) and then build there a vast pavilion fit for heaven and adorn it with her own jewels. Then I invite all the angels and saints to come and sing hymns of love. It seems to me that Jesus is pleased to see Himself received with such magnificence. I share His delight. But it doesn't prevent me from being distracted and feeling sleepy. So I often resolve to continue my thanksgiving throughout the whole day, as I've made it so badly.

So you see that the path I tread is far from the way of fear. I always know how to be happy in spite of my failings and to profit from them.

Holiness

Holiness is not a matter of any one particular method of
spirituality: it is a disposition of the heart that makes us
small and humble within the arms of God, aware of our
weakness, but almost rashly confident in His Fatherly
goodness.

42

Thérèse's Spirit of Poverty

—Process testimony of her sister Marie

Sister Thérèse of the Child Jesus constantly practiced poverty without ever complaining. From her beginnings in Carmel, when she was only fifteen years old, she was treated without the slightest consideration. One said to the cook, "Nobody will eat that; give it to Sister Thérèse of the Child Jesus who never says no to anything." So one would see reappear in her plate toward the end of the week omelette that had been cooked the previous Sunday [this in days before refrigeration]. At table she shared, with another sister who sat next to her, some cider contained in a bottle so small that it could hardly have held two glassfuls. She drank nothing, in order not to deprive this neighbor. She could have taken some water from the jug but she held back in order that no one notice her mortification and act of charity [in leaving the cider].

Out of a spirit of poverty, she didn't reclaim what others took from her, saying nothing belonged to her; and the gifts of intelligence, which God had given her in such abundance, she let, in a manner of speaking, be stolen: at recreation, if another repeated something Thérèse had said as if it was the second person's thought or clever phrase, Thérèse let the honor go to the other without making known what was the [true] source.

A Little Beggar

44

One must say to the good God: "I know very well that I will never be worthy of what I hope for, but I am holding out my hand to You like a little beggar and I'm sure that You will respond fully to my desires because You are so good!"

Her "Little Way" to Heaven

I've always wanted to become a saint. Unfortunately, I've always found the same difference between the saints and me as there is between a mountain and a humble grain of sand. [But] instead of being discouraged, I told myself: God would not make me wish for something impossible. It is impossible for me to grow bigger, so I put up with myself as I am, with all my countless faults. But I will look for some means of going to heaven by a little way which is very short and very straight.

We live in an age of inventions. We need no longer climb laboriously up flights of stairs. And I am determined to find an elevator to carry me to Jesus, for I was too small to climb the steep stairs of perfection. So I sought in Holy Scripture some idea of what this lift I wanted would be, and I read, "Whoever is a little one, let him come to Me." I also wanted to know how God would deal with a "little one," so I [searched] and found: "You shall be carried at the breasts and upon knees; as one whom the mother caresses...."

It is your arms, Jesus, which are the elevator to carry me to heaven. So there is no need for me to grow up. In fact, just the opposite: I must become less and less.

To Reach the Summit of Love

46

Jesus has shown me the only path which leads to the divine furnace of love. It is the complete abandonment of a baby sleeping without fear in its father's arms.

[None should] despair of reaching the summit of love, since Jesus does not ask for great actions but only abandonment and gratitude. "Offer to God sacrifices of praise and thanksgiving."

That is all Jesus asks from us. He has no need of our works but only of our *love*. God does not hesitate to *beg* a drop of water from the woman of Samaria. He was thirsty!!! But the Creator of the universe was asking for the love of the poor thing He had created. He was thirsty for love! And now more than ever Jesus thirsts. Even among His disciples there are very few who surrender fully to the tenderness of His infinite love.

The Science of Love

—To her sister Marie

Don't imagine that I'm overwhelmed with consolations. I'm not. My consolation is to not have any. Jesus never manifests Himself nor lets me hear His voice. He teaches me in secret. I never learn anything from books, for I don't understand what I read. Yet from time to time a sentence comforts me. This evening, after a barren period of meditation, I read this: "Here is the Master I give you. He will teach you all you need to do. I want to make you read of the *science of love* in the book of life."

The science of love! The words echo sweetly through my soul. It is the only thing I want to know. Like the spouse in the Canticle of Canticles, "having given up all the substance of my house for love, I reckon it as nothing." I long for no other treasure but love, for it alone can make us pleasing to God.

It Is Easy to Give When Asked Nicely

48

Jesus teaches me: "Give to everyone that asketh thee, and of him that taketh away thy goods, ask them not again."

It is not so pleasant to give to one who asks as it is to offer something freely and spontaneously; and it is easy to give when asked nicely, but if asked tactlessly, we at once want to refuse unless perfect charity strengthens us. We find a thousand reasons for saying no, and it is not until we have made the sister aware of her bad manners that we give her what she wants *as a favor*, or do her a slight service taking a quarter of the time spent telling her of the obstacles preventing our doing it or of our fancied rights.

And it is that much harder to let what belongs to us be taken without asking for it back. But the moment we accept this, we feel how light [the burden] is.

The Truly Poor in Spirit

I used to believe I had no possessiveness about anything but since I have really grasped what Jesus means, I see how far I am from being perfect. If, for example, I start painting and find the brushes in a mess, or a ruler or a penknife gone, I very nearly lose my patience and have to hold onto it with both hands to prevent my asking bad-temperedly for them. Of course I can ask for these essential tools and I do not disobey Jesus if I ask *humbly*, like poor people who hold out their hands for the necessities of life [knowing] no one owes them anything. What peace pours over the soul once it soars above natural feelings! There is no joy like that known by the truly poor in spirit.

What Vowed Poverty Truly Means

One evening after compline, I looked in vain for my lamp on the shelves where they are kept. As it was the Lent Silence, I couldn't ask for it. I thought—rightly—that a sister had taken it in mistake for hers. So, because of this mistake, I had to spend a whole hour in darkness and it was an evening when I'd planned to do a lot of work. But for the interior light of grace, I should certainly have been very sorry for myself. As it was, instead of feeling upset, I rejoiced and thought that true poverty meant being without essentials, not only without pleasant things.

The Hidden Depths of Charity

When He tells me, "Give to everyone that asks of you and don't ask to have your goods back when someone takes them from you," I think He is speaking not only of material possessions but also of spiritual treasures. By the vow of poverty I renounced the first and the others are also lent by God. He can take them and I have no right to grumble. Yet our thoughts, our ardent ideas and feelings seem a treasure which no one has a right to touch. If I tell a sister about some enlightenment that came to me in prayer and she later discloses it as if it were hers, I'm inclined to think she has stolen my property. Or if during recreation one whispers something amusing to her neighbor and she repeats it aloud without saying where it came from, that strikes its author as theft. She may say nothing [then], but at the first opportunity she will delicately make known that her ideas were stolen.

I have suffered these pathetic human failings myself. Now I can say that I am no more attached to my own ideas or feelings than to material possessions. I find it quite natural that the other sisters grab [my ideas if they like them] for such are the Holy Ghost's, not mine.

Her Heroic Obedience

52

—Process testimony of Thérèse and Pauline's oldest sister, Marie

She confided that the Prioress had permitted Mother Agnes of Jesus (Thérèse's sister Pauline) to sometimes have a talk with her [Thérèse]. These became for Thérèse occasions of great sacrifice, because, not having received on her side permission to reveal her intimate thoughts [to Pauline] she restricted herself to simply hearing the confidences of the one she called "her little mother" without returning any confidences of her own. Yet she would have had only to say a word to obtain the permission. "But," she said, "it's not necessary to get oneself given permissions which will sweeten the martyrdom of religious life, because then it would be just a natural life and without merit."

Love for Family Deepens When Purified

I did not enter Carmel to live with my sisters*; on the contrary. I clearly foresaw how much I should suffer when I could not give way to my natural affection for them. I do not understand people saying that it is holier to keep aloof from one's relatives. No one ever blames brothers for fighting side by side on the same battlefield or for winning the palm of martyrdom together. It is quite true they encourage each other, but the sufferings of one hurt all the others. It is exactly the same in life in religion, that life which theologians call a martyrdom. To offer oneself to God does not mean that one loses anything at all of one's natural tenderness. It is just the opposite, for this tenderness deepens as it becomes purified by centering on divine things. I am glad to fight as one of a family for the glory of God, but I am also ready to depart to another battlefield if He wishes. [There had been talk of Thérèse being sent to a Carmel in Vietnam before her illness made this impossible.]

* Her two oldest sisters, Marie and Pauline, were in the Lisieux Carmel when Thérèse entered. Later her cousin Marie and Céline, the sister closest in age to Thérèse, also entered there.

Loving Others in God

54

—Thérèse writes to Mother Marie de Gonzague, the prioress

I remember that when I was a postulant I sometimes longed to seek my own satisfaction and enjoy a little pleasure. This longing was so strong that I was forced to hurry past your cell and to clutch the balustrade to prevent myself turning back. A thousand excuses for seeing you came into my head so that I could justify my natural impulses—excuses like asking your permission for various things. How glad I am now that I crushed such impulses right from the start of my religious life! I am already enjoying the reward promised to those who fight bravely. No longer do I feel that I must refuse to let my heart have any comfort, for my heart is centered on God. Because it has loved only Him, it has gradually developed until it can manifest to those dear to Him a tenderness incomparably deeper than if it had spent itself in selfish, barren love.

How Sweet a Joy That God Is Just

I know that every soul cannot be alike. There must be different kinds so that each of the perfections of God can be specially honored. To me, He has revealed His infinite mercy, and I see all His other attributes in the light of that. Thus they all seem glowing with love: His justice, perhaps even more than the others, is clothed with love, for how sweet a joy it is to think that God is just, that, in other words, He makes allowances for our weaknesses and understands perfectly the frailty of our humanity. So what have I to be afraid of? If God, who is perfectly just, shows such mercy in forgiving the prodigal son, must He not also be *just* to me "who am always with Him"?

Confidence in His Mercy

56

O Jesus, I feel that if You found a soul feebler than mine—though that's impossible—You would delight in heaping even greater favors on it, if it abandoned itself with supreme confidence to Your infinite mercy.

Jesus Teaches Without Words

I have had great enlightenment from the writings of St. John of the Cross. When I was between seventeen and eighteen, they were my only spiritual food. But as I grew older, religious writers left me quite unmoved. I'm still like that. If I glance at a book, no matter how good and moving it is, my heart at once contracts and I read without understanding or, if I understand, I cannot meditate on it. When I'm in this state, the Bible and *The Imitation [of Christ]* come to my rescue. In them I find hidden manna, a pure and substantial food. But, above all, the Gospels help me in my prayers. They are always showing me new ways of looking at things, and I am always finding hidden and mysterious meanings in them. I understand and, by experience, I know that the Kingdom of God is within us. Jesus has no need of books of Doctors of the Church to guide souls. He, the Doctor of Doctors, can teach without words. I have never heard Him speak, but I know that He is within me. He guides and inspires me every moment of the day. Just when I need it, a new light shines on my problems.

The Farther One Travels...

58

At the start of my spiritual life, when I was thirteen or fourteen, I used to wonder what more I could ever learn about spiritual perfection. I thought it impossible to understand it better. But I soon came to know that the farther one travels along that road, the farther away the goal seems to get. Nowadays I'm resigned to seeing myself in a permanent state of imperfection and I even delight in it.

What Prayer Is

For me, prayer means launching out from the heart toward God; a cry of grateful love from the crest of joy or the trough of despair: it is a vast supernatural force that opens out my heart and binds me close to Jesus.

59

Confidence in God's Loving Mercy

It is not because I have been preserved from mortal sin that I fly to God with loving confidence. I know I should still have this confidence even if my conscience were burdened with every possible crime. I should fling myself into the arms of my Savior, heartbroken with sorrow. I know how He loved the prodigal son, I have heard his words to St. Mary Magdalene, to the woman taken in adultery, and to the woman of Samaria. No, no one could frighten me, for I know what to think about His love and His mercy. I know that a host of sins would vanish in the twinkling of an eye, like a drop of water flung into a furnace.

The Key to Her Vocation

It should be enough for me, Jesus, to be a Carmelite and, by union with You, the mother of souls. Yet I long for other vocations: I want to be a warrior, a priest, an apostle, a Doctor of the Church, a martyr. I should like to enlighten souls. I should like to wander the world, preaching Your Name. Nor should I be content to be a missionary for only a few years; I should like to [be] one till the end of time.

These desires caused me a real martyrdom [until I found] chapters 12-13 of First Corinthians and read that we cannot all be apostles, doctors, etc. I went on reading: "Be zealous for the better gifts. And I show unto you a yet more excellent way." Charity gave me the key to *my vocation*. I realized that love includes all vocations, is in all things, and because it is eternal, embraces every time and place.

My vocation is love! It is You, Lord, who has given it to me. [So] in the heart of the Church *I will be love*. [You, Lord] will descend to [my] nothingness and transform that nothingness into living fire.

Céline: Sister and Spiritual Companion

—From a letter dated April 26, 1892

62

Céline, you alone can understand my language; in the eyes of creatures, our life seems very different, very much separated*, but I know that our treasure is Jesus and our hearts make one in Him.

* Thérèse was already a nun and Céline, an attractive single woman, was caring for their ill father.

The Call to Save Souls by Prayer

—Letter to Céline dated August 15, 1892

63

I was thinking of what I could do to save souls [and] a word of the gospel gave me a real light. Jesus said to His disciples: "Lift up your eyes and see...the fields [ready]...to harvest" and a little later: "In truth, the harvest is abundant but laborers few; ask the master to send laborers." What a mystery! Is not Jesus all-powerful? Ah, it is because Jesus has so incomprehensible a love for us that He wills that we have a share with Him in the salvation of souls. He wills to do nothing without us. The Creator of the Universe awaits the prayer of a poor little soul to save other souls redeemed like it at the price of all, His blood.

[Some will harvest, but Thérèse and Céline are to be prayer warriors.] These are the words of our Jesus: "*Lift* your eyes. See how in My heaven there are empty places; it is up to you to fill them: you are My Moses praying on the mountain; ask Me for workers and I shall send them. I await only a prayer from your heart."

Our mission as Carmelites is to form evangelical workers who will save thousands of souls. Céline, if these were not the very words of our Jesus, who would dare to believe in them?

She Can "Split Your Sides With Laughter"

—Sketch of Thérèse by her novice mistress, Sister Marie of the Angels, written in 1893

Thérèse of the Child Jesus, twenty years old. Novice and jewel of the Carmel; its dear Benjamin. Office of painting in which she excels without having had any other lessons than those of seeing our Reverend Mother, her dear sister, at work. Tall and strong, with the appearance of a child, a tone of voice, an expression, hiding within her a wisdom, a perfection, a perspicacity of a fifty-year-old. Soul always calm and in perfect possession of itself in all things and with everybody. Little innocent thing, to whom one would give God without confession, but whose head is full of mischief to play on anyone she pleases. Mystic, comic, everything—she can make you weep with devotion and just as easily split your sides with laughter during our recreations.

Give, With No Thought of Results!

65

—Working with the Carmelite novices

I throw to the right and the left to my little birds the good seed that the good God puts in my little hand. And then, the seed does what it will! I don't concern myself about it. Sometimes the results are as if I had thrown nothing; other times, something good results. But the good God says to me, "Give, give always without concerning yourself with results."

A Novice's Testimony

—Sister Marie of the Eucharist was Thérèse's cousin Marie Guerin*

66

Ah! How many times she spoke these words to me: "I beg you, be busied a little less with yourself, occupy yourself with loving God, and forget about yourself. All your scruples, these are just a lot of self-seeking. Your griefs, your sorrows—all that is centered on yourself: it is like spinning around on the same pivot. Ah! I beg you, forget yourself; think of saving souls."

* Thérèse cured this cousin and former playmate of scruples while Marie was a lay-woman; when Marie became a Carmelite, Thérèse gave her the spiritual direction that set her on the road to holiness.

How to Force Jesus to Help You

67

—To novice Sister Martha of Jesus

Dear little Sister, yes, I understood all. I am begging Jesus to make the sun of His grace shine in your soul. Ah! Do not fear to tell Him you *love Him even without feeling it*. This is the way *to force* Jesus to help you, to carry you like a little child too feeble to walk.

It is a great trial to look on the *black* side, but this does not depend on you completely. Do what you *can*; detach your heart from the *worries* of this earth, and above all from creatures, and then be sure Jesus will do the *rest*. He will be unable to allow you to fall into the dreaded *mire*. Be consoled, dear little Sister, in heaven you will no longer *take a dark view of everything* but *a very bright view*. Yes, everything will be decked out in the divine brightness of our Spouse [Jesus].

A Failure*

—Pauline, renamed Mother Agnes of Jesus in Carmel, was one of the saint's two prioresses. Pauline wrote to relatives:

I could not make you understand to what a degree Sister Marie-Madeleine [one of the novices under Thérèse's spiritual care] is estranged from Sister Thérèse of the Child Jesus, because she [the novice] feels herself read to the very depths of her soul, and is obliged, as a consequence, to wage war against her [unruly] nature. When I was prioress, I had obligated her for a period of one year to go to Thérèse for one half-hour on Sundays, and I know what [ensued].

[Sister Marie-Madeleine herself testified under oath after Thérèse's death]: When she [Thérèse] told me to go with her at an hour agreed upon, I often used to go and hide instead of going with her. Then she would look for me and when she could not find me and we later met, she would say: "I looked for you and I could not find you." I would answer coldly: "I was busy." In these circumstances, she retained her calm and smiling face.

---

* After Thérèse's death, she so succeeded in changing Marie-Madeleine that the latter claimed to no longer recognize herself.

On Helping Souls

69

All my strength lies in prayer and sacrifice. They are my invincible weapons, and I know, by experience, that they can soften the heart much better than words.

The Truth, Come What May!

I was quite little when my aunt read me a story which
astonished me greatly. I saw, from it, that a schoolmistress
was praised because she knew how to adroitly extricate herself from matters without wounding anyone. I was especially
struck by the phrase: "She said to this one: You're not wrong; and
to that one: You're right." And I thought to myself: this isn't good!
This individual ought to have not feared anything and told to her
pupils that they were wrong when that was true.

And today I haven't changed my opinion. I have a lot more trouble [than she], I admit, because it's always so easy to put the blame
on those who are absent, and that calms right away the one who's
complaining. But I do completely the contrary. If I am not loved
[because of it] so what! I tell the whole truth, so let them not seek
me out, unless they wish to hear it.

A Little Bitterness

71

God has given me the grace of having no fear of a fight. I will do my duty at any cost. More than once I have been told [by novices she was giving spiritual direction]: "If you want to succeed with me, severity is no use. You will get nowhere unless you are gentle." But I know that no one is a good judge in his own case. If a surgeon performs a painful operation on a child, the child will scream and say that the cure is worse than the disease. But after a few days when he is cured, he is delighted to be able to run about and play. It is exactly the same where souls are concerned. They soon realize that a little bitterness is better than sweetness.

Goodness vs. Weakness

Goodness should not degenerate into weakness. When one has scolded someone justly, it's necessary to let it alone, without letting oneself soften to the point of self torment over having given pain, seeing someone suffer and weep. To run after the pained one in order to console her would be to do her more harm than good. Leaving her to herself is to force her to run to the good God in order to see her wrong and humble herself. To do otherwise, habituating her to receive consolation after a merited scolding, would be to make her always act thusly in similar circumstances, like a spoiled infant who dances about in a rage crying until its mother comes to dry its tears.

72

On Her Charity and Serenity

—Process testimony of her sister Marie

73

During recreations she would have been able often to find a seat near us (her older sisters, Pauline and Marie), but she preferred to seek the company of those who called for exercising the most charity. She never let herself show anger at harsh words said to her. One day [in 1891], when she was arranging as best she could some bouquets sent to put around the coffin of Mother Genevieve, one of the lay sisters said to her: "It's easy to see which flowers come from your family, since you put them right out front, while those of poor folk you scorn." I wondered how Thérèse was going to reply to such unjust words; but she looked at this sister in the most loving way and immediately gave way to her desire, putting the least beautiful flowers out front.

When she had charge of the novices [beginning in 1893], one day I saw a young postulant heap reproaches on her, saying some very hard things to her. Sister Thérèse kept her calm perfectly, but I guessed at the extreme violence she had to do to herself to listen with such serenity to such biting words.

Heroic Humility

The novices [whom she gave spiritual direction] praise me. It is not flattery. They believe what they say. [It] does not make me vain, for the knowledge of my wretchedness never leaves me. But sometimes my soul sickens of too sweet a diet. It is then that Jesus gives me a nice little salad [dressing] of vinegar and spice *sans* olive oil.

74

God raises the veil which hides my imperfections and my dear little sisters then no longer find me quite to their liking. With a simplicity I find charming, they tell me what a trial I am to them and what they find unpleasant about me. They stand on no ceremony, for they know that their freedom of speech delights me.

It is actually more than delight. It is like a wonderful festival which overwhelms me with joy. If I had not experienced it, I could not believe that something so against one's natural feelings could afford such happiness.

Once when I was passionately longing to be humiliated, a young postulant did it so effectively that I remembered when Semei cursed David and I repeated the words of the holy king: "Yea, it is the Lord who hath bidden him say all these things."

Keeping the Fire of Love Burning

—From July 18, 1893 letter to Céline

75

God is no longer asking anything from me [after earlier] asking an infinity of things. [So] I thought I had [only] to go along quietly in peace and love. But I had an insight: St. Teresa says we must maintain love. *The wood* is not within our reach when we are in darkness, in aridities, but at least are we not obligated to throw little pieces of straw on [the fire of love]? Jesus is, it's true, powerful enough to keep the fire going by Himself. However He is happy when He sees us put a little fuel on it—this *attentiveness* pleases Him and then He throws on a lot of wood. We do not see it but we feel the *strength* of love's warmth. I have experienced it: when I am *feeling* nothing, when I am *incapable of praying*, of practicing virtue, then is the moment for seeking opportunities, *nothings* which please Jesus more than mastery of the world when suffered with generosity. For example, a smile, a friendly word, when I would want to say nothing, or put on a look of annoyance, etc.

Céline, do you understand? It is not for the purpose of gaining merits; it is in order to please Jesus.

God Is Content With Good Will

—From November 17, 1893 letter to her aunt*

When I am before the tabernacle, I can say only one thing to Our Lord: "My God, you know that I love You." And I feel my prayer does not tire Jesus; knowing the helplessness of His poor little spouse, He is content with her good will.

76

---

* Céline Guerin was married to the brother of Thérèse's mother. When Zélie died, although they had two young daughters of their own, Céline and her husband took a great interest in the rearing of their five motherless nieces, particularly the two youngest: Céline (her aunt's namesake) and Thérèse.

Consoling Jesus

—*From July 7, 1894 letter to Céline*

77

How sweet it will be to hear one day from the mouth of our Jesus: "You are the ones who have always remained with Me in all the trials I have had." The trials of Jesus, what a mystery! He has trials then, He too? Yes, He has them, and often He is alone. He looks for consolers and can find none. Many serve Jesus when He is consoling them, but *few* consent to keep company with *Jesus sleeping* on the waves or suffering in the garden of agony! Who, then, will be willing to serve Jesus for Himself? Ah! We shall be the ones. Céline and Thérèse will unite always more and more; in them, will be accomplished this prayer of Jesus: "Father, that they may be one as we are one." [Jesus said,] "If anyone loves me, he will keep my word." But what then is this word? It seems to me that the *word* of Jesus is *Himself*. He, *Jesus*, the *Word of God!* He tells us in the same Gospel of St. John, praying to the Father for His disciples: "Sanctify them by your *word*, your word is *truth*." In another place Jesus teaches us that He is the way, the *truth*, the life. We know then, what is the *Word* that we must keep: Jesus in our hearts!

Infinite Love

—From July 16, 1894 letter to a young married friend

Oh! how beautiful is our religion; instead of contracting hearts (as the world believes), it raises them up and renders them capable of *loving*, or *loving* with a love *almost infinite*, since this love must continue after this mortal life which is given to us only for meriting the homeland of heaven where we shall find again the dear ones whom we have loved on earth!

[In her last message to this same woman, sent verbally through another nun as Thérèse lay dying, Thérèse urges her married contemporary]: "God is calling you to be a real saint in the world...."

78

What God Wants

—From July 18, 1894 letter to Céline

79

Frequently God wants only *our will*; He asks *all*, and if we were to refuse Him the least thing, He loves us too much to give in to us; however, as soon as our will is conformed to His, as soon as He sees we seek Him alone, then He conducts Himself with us as in the past He conducted Himself with Abraham, [who was asked to sacrifice his beloved son; when God saw Abraham willing to offer even his best beloved, God canceled the request].

On the Death of Her Father on July 29, 1894

—From August 20th letter to Léonie

80

I'm thinking more than ever about you, since our dear father departed for heaven. Papa's death didn't have on me the effect of a death but of a true life. I find him again after six years of absence. I sense him around me, looking at me and protecting me. Dear little sister,* aren't we more united now that we look to the heavens to find the father and mother who offered us to Jesus?

* A term of affection: Leonie is actually ten years older.

The Folly and Foolishness of God

—From August 19, 1894 letter to Céline

81

We have only the short moment of this life to *give* to God, and He is already preparing to say: "Now, my turn." What a joy to suffer for Him who loves us unto *folly* and to pass as *fools* in the eyes of the world. Yes, it was *folly* to seek out the poor little hearts of mortals to make them His *thrones*, He the King of Glory, who is seated above the Cherubim. He, whom the heavens cannot contain. He was *foolish*, our Beloved, to come to earth in search of sinners in order to make them His friends, His intimates, His *equals*—He who was perfectly happy with the two adorable persons of the Trinity!

The Rejected Love of God

In 1895 I was enabled to understand more clearly how Jesus longs to be loved. I was thinking of those souls who offer themselves as victims to the justice of God, so that, by drawing it down on themselves, they turn aside the punishment due to sinners. From the depths of my heart, I cried: "O my divine Master, must it be only Your justice which has its victims? Hasn't Your merciful love need of them too? It is everywhere rejected and ignored. Those on whom You long to lavish it seek a wretched, fleeting happiness in other creatures instead of flinging themselves into Your arms and welcoming the flames of Your divine love. Must Your rejected love stay shut up in Your Heart? It seems to me that if you found souls offering themselves as sacrificial victims of Your love, You would consume them speedily and would rejoice to unloose those torrents of infinite tenderness You hold within Yourself. If your justice must spend itself how much more must Your merciful love long to inflame souls. O Jesus, let me be Your eager victim and consume Your little sacrifice in the fire of divine love."

Thérèse's Act of Oblation

[Thérèse's oldest sister, Marie, recalled years later that in 1895, when they were working with the hay in Carmel's meadow, Thérèse had asked her if she wanted to offer herself as a victim to the Merciful Love of God and that she answered]: "'Certainly not. I am not going to offer myself as a victim; God would take me at my word, and suffering frightens me too much. In the first place, this word "victim" displeases me very much.' Then little Thérèse answered that she understood me, but that to offer oneself as a victim to God's Love was not at all the same as offering oneself to His justice, that I would not suffer more, that it was in order to be able to love God better for those who do not want to love Him. She was so eloquent that I allowed her to win me over, and I am not sorry either!"

The Dream of Three Carmelites

I dreamed I saw three Carmelites, wearing their mantles and long veils. I knew they were from heaven. "How happy I should be," I thought, "to see the face of one of them." The tallest lifted her veil. I recognized Venerable Mother Anne of Jesus, foundress of Carmel in France. Her face had a beauty not of earth.

She caressed me and, moved by her love, I asked: "I implore you, Mother, to tell me if God is going to come for me soon? She gave me a tender smile:

"Yes, soon."

I went on: "Tell me also, Mother, if God is pleased with me. Does He want anything from me beyond my poor little deeds and longings?"

Her gaze grew even more tender. She said: "God asks nothing more from you. He is pleased, very pleased." She took my head between her hands and I cannot give any idea of the sweetness of her love. I was aflame with joy.

[Since this dream] I believe and I know heaven exists and souls dwell there who love me and look upon me as their child. The realization was all the sweeter because until then I had been quite indifferent to Venerable Anne of Jesus. Now I know she is far from indifferent about me. This knowledge deepens my love both for her and for all the blessed ones in heaven.

Thérèse's Courage

—Process testimony of her sister Marie

At the time of the trials with our father, it was Sister Thérèse who kept up our courage. Seeing her so strong, one didn't even bother about her [feelings].

She showed also great strength in [her] daily mortifications. For example, when dinner consisted of beans: She was given a big portion, and not knowing they made her sick, our [prioress] strongly recommended she eat whatever was served; she was made ill each time. But she never said anything about it and only confided this to us when she was in the infirmary.

Her courage of soul also manifested itself *vis-à-vis* a sister for whom she felt a great antipathy, as she says in her autobiography. Thinking, on the contrary, that she loved this sister greatly, I was jealous and I said to her one day: "I can't keep from telling you an irritation I have. I feel that you like Sister—better than you like me. And I find that unjust since the good Lord made family ties. You greet her with more signs of pleasure than you ever show about being with me." She laughed heartily but she didn't confide [in me.] Good Friday night 1896 she coughed up blood. I met her in the morning, pale and exhausted, but she never said a word about [it].

Her Great Trial of Faith

—Beginning at Easter 1896

The very desires and intuitions of my inmost heart assured me that another and more lovely land awaited me, an abiding city. Then suddenly Jesus allowed pitch-black darkness to sweep over my soul for months. [I] am still waiting for it to end. It is a sunless tunnel [where] the voice of unbelievers mocks me out of the darkness: "You dream of light, of a fragrant land; you dream that their Creator will be yours forever. Hope on! And look forward to death! But it will give you, not what you hope for, but a still darker night, the night of annihilation." He knows very well that although I haven't the consolation of faith, I force myself to act as if I had. I have made more acts of faith in the last year than in the whole of my life. I sing very strongly in my heart: "After death life is immortal." What darkness! But I dwell there in peace [even though] the veil of faith is no longer a veil; it is a wall, shutting out the stars. When I sing of heaven's happiness, of what it is to possess God forever, I feel no joy; I simply sing of what I want to believe.*

---

* Yet during this dark night, Thérèse made all her astounding prophecies about the work she would do after death—every one of which has come true!

A Heart Full of Loving Tact

—From April 11, 1896 letter to her sister Léonie, who three times tried to become a nun, and three times failed

Dear little sister, how sweet it is that we can, all five, call Jesus "Our Beloved." But what will it be when we shall see Him in heaven and follow Him everywhere, singing the same canticle only virgins are permitted to sing!

Then we shall understand the value of suffering, and, like Jesus, we shall repeat: "It was really necessary that suffering should try us and have us come to glory."

Dear little sister, I cannot tell you all the deep thoughts my heart contains concerning yourself; the only thing I want to say is this: I love you a thousand times more tenderly than ordinary sisters love each other, for I can love you with the *Heart* of our celestial Spouse.

In Him we are living the same life....

"Taking Hold of Jesus by His Heart"

—From July 12, 1896 letter to Léonie

I assure you that God is much better than you believe. He is content with a glance, a sigh of love. As for me, I find perfection very easy to practice because I have understood it as a matter of *taking hold of Jesus by His Heart*. Look at a little child who has just annoyed his mother. If he hides away in a corner in a sulky mood and in fear of being punished his mamma will not pardon him. But if he comes to her, holding out his little arms, smiling, and saying: "Kiss me, I will not do it again," will his mother be able not to press him to her heart tenderly and forget his childish mischief? However, she knows her dear little one *will do it again* on the next occasion, but this does not matter; if he takes her again *by her heart*, he will not be punished.*

---

* Thérèse writes from one or more experiences of this forbearance from her birth mother.

Jesus Pays the Fares

—From July 12 letter to Léonie, while suffering with tuberculosis

89

You ask me news of my health. Well, my dear little sister, I'm not coughing anymore at all—are you happy? That won't keep the good Lord from taking me when He desires, since I'm making every effort to be wholly a little child: I have no preparations [therefore] to make: Jesus must Himself pay all the fares for the trip and the price for entrance to heaven!

The Danger of Quick Judgments

Ah, how necessary it is not to judge anything on earth. Here's what happened to me during recreation several months ago. It was a nothing, but it taught me a lot.

Two bells rang and the [nun whose job it was to answer] being absent, it fell to Sister Thérèse of St. Augustine to go to the turn. Ordinarily this is boring, but this time it was tempting since one was to open the door in order to receive the branches for the creche.

Sister Marie of St. Joseph was beside me and I guessed that she shared my child's desire. "Who wants to help with me the turn?" said Sister Thérèse of St. Augustine. At once I undid my apron, but slowly, so that Sister Marie of St. Joseph would be ready before and take the spot, which is what happened.

Then, laughing and looking at me, Sister Thérèse of St. Augustine said, "Well, it's Sister Marie of St. Joseph who'll have this pearl in her crown. You were too slow."

I made no reply except for a smile and went back to my work, saying to myself: "O Lord, how different are your judgments from those of people! How often on earth we deceive ourselves, taking for imperfection in our sisters what is valued by you."

"Blind Hope in His Mercy"

—From September 17, 1896 letter to Marie

[Marie has written Thérèse that she wishes to love God as much as Thérèse, who longs for martyrdom for His sake, while Marie shrinks from such thoughts. Thérèse replies:]

My desires of martyrdom *are nothing*; they are, to tell the truth, the spiritual riches that *render one unjust* when one rests in them with complacence believ[ing] they are *something great*. These desires are a *consolation* that Jesus grants at times to weak souls like mine (and these souls are numerous). Recall those words of Father [Pichon]: "The martyrs suffered with joy and the King of Martyrs suffered with sadness." Yes, Jesus said: "Father, let this chalice pass away...." How can you say after this that my desires are the sign of my [greater] love? I really feel that what pleases Him is *that He sees me loving my littleness and my poverty, the blind hope that I have in His mercy*. That is my only treasure. Why would this treasure not be yours?

Are you not ready to suffer all that God will desire? I know you are; therefore, if you want to feel joy it is your consolation you are seeking. I assure you, if we were to go to martyrdom in the dispositions we are in now, you would have great merit and I would have none at all.

Raising a Little the Mysterious Veil

—From November 1, 1896 reply to a letter from Father Roulland, a missionary her prioress asks her to support by prayer

[When Thérèse became a Carmelite she asked God, since she could not be a priest, that He give her "an apostolic soul"— "a priest"—who would in her place, "receive the graces of the Lord" for missionary work. Now she has discovered that this young missionary priest's vocation was saved September 8, 1890, the day Thérèse made this request as she vowed her life to God as a Carmelite prayer warrior. After explaining all this, her letter continues:]

I believed I would meet only in heaven the apostle, the brother whom I had asked from Jesus; but this Beloved Savior, raising a little the mysterious veil that hides the secrets of eternity, has seen fit to give me in this exile the consolation of knowing the brother of my soul, of working with him for the salvation of [souls].

How great is my gratitude. What is He reserving for us in heaven if here below His love dispenses surprises so delightful?

More than ever, I understand that the smallest events of our life are conducted by God; He is the One who makes us desire and who grants our desires.

How Sweet Is the Way of Love!

I wish for only one thing: to love Jesus even unto folly! Love alone attracts me. I no longer wish for either suffering or death and yet both are precious to me. For a long time I've hailed them as messengers of joy. I've already known suffering and I've thought I was approaching the eternal shore. From my earliest days I have believed [I'd] be plucked in the springtime of life. But today my only guide is self-abandonment. I no longer know how to ask passionately for anything except that the will of God shall be perfectly accomplished in my soul. I can repeat the words of our Father, St. John of the Cross: "I drank deep within the hidden cellar of my Beloved and, when I came forth again, I remembered nothing of the flock I used to look after. I've finished all other work except that of love. In that is all my delight."

How sweet is the way of love! Of course one may stumble and be guilty of small faults, but love, able to draw good from everything, will very quickly destroy all that displeases Jesus and will fill one's heart with a deep and humble peace.

Words! Inadequate Words!

—From November 16, 1896 letter to Thérèse's aunt

94

It is very sad for your poor little daughter* to be obliged to entrust a cold pen with the care of expressing the sentiments of her heart. Perhaps you will say with a smile: "But, little Thérèse, would you express them more easily in words?" Dear Aunt, I have to admit it, no, it is true, I do not find expressions that satisfy the aspirations of my heart.

The poet who dared to say:

"What is well understood is clearly expressed,

And the words to express it come with ease …,"

[this poet] did not feel what I feel in the depths of my soul!!!

Fortunately, I have the deep Father Faber** to console me. He understood that words and sentences here below are incapable of expressing feelings of the heart and *full* hearts are the ones containing the most within themselves.

---

* Thérèse refers to herself as her aunt's daughter as a mark of gratitude for her loving help in Thérèse's rearing.

** a well-known spiritual writer

How Consoling That Jesus Trembled

—From December 26, 1896 letter to Father Belliere, the
second missionary Thérèse supports with prayer

I assure you I am doing all that is within my power to
obtain the graces necessary for you; these graces certainly will
be granted to you since Our Lord never asks sacrifices from us
above our strength. At times, it is true, this divine Savior makes us
feel all the bitterness of the chalice that He is offering our soul.
When He asks the sacrifice of all that is dearest in this world, it is
impossible, without a very special grace, not to cry out like Him in
the garden of agony: "Father, let this chalice pass from me—however, may Your will be done and not mine."

It is very consoling to think that Jesus, the Strong God,[15] knew
our weaknesses, that He trembled at the sight of the bitter chalice,
this chalice that He had in the past so ardently desired to drink.[16]

---

* See Isaiah 9:5
** See Luke 22:15

To Do Good on Earth From Heaven!

—*Testimony of her oldest sister, Marie*

96

I recall that on the feast of St. Joseph [March 19, 1897] I was in his hermitage. Thérèse came there, and she was quite ill. I told her that she would have done much better to go directly to her cell than to take this roundabout way. She told me: "I am coming to ask St. Joseph to obtain from God the grace for me to spend my heaven in doing good on earth." I answered: "You do not have to ask this from St. Joseph." But she said "Oh! yes" with a gesture which meant I need him to support my request. She had also asked this [prayer support] from St. Francis Xavier [patron of the missions].

[Thérèse herself put in the mouth of St. Stanislaus Kostka—in a piece she wrote to celebrate the anniversary of solemn vows by a nun who took this saint's name—the plea:]

"I have a desire, a desire so great that I shall be unable to be happy in heaven if it is not realized. Tell me whether the blessed can still work for the salvation of souls. If I cannot work in paradise for the glory of Jesus, I prefer to remain in [this] exile."

God Remembers We Are but Dust

—From May 9, 1897 letter to Father Roulland

I know that the Lord is infinitely just; and it is this justice, which frightens so many souls, that is the object of my joy and confidence. To be just is not only to exercise severity in order to punish the guilty; it is also to recognize right intentions and to reward virtue. I expect as much from God's justice as from His mercy. It is because He is just that "He is compassionate and filled with gentleness, slow to punish, and abundant in mercy, for He knows our frailty, He remembers we are only dust. As a father has tenderness for his children, so the Lord has compassion on us!"

Oh, Brother, when hearing these beautiful and consoling words of the Prophet-King, how can we doubt that God will open the doors of His kingdom to His children who loved Him.

The Power of Scripture

—From May 1897 letter to Father Roulland

98

At times, when I am reading certain spiritual treatises in which perfection is shown through a thousand obstacles, surrounded by a crowd of illusions, my poor little mind quickly tires. I close the learned book that leaves my head splitting and my heart parched, and I pick up the Holy Scriptures. Then all seems luminous—a single word opens up infinite horizons to my soul.

On Praying for Others

99

I am especially united to the new brothers [Fathers Roulland and Belliere, young missionaries her Prioress asked Thérèse to support with prayer,] given me by Jesus.

All I have belongs equally to each of them, for God is too good and generous to divide it. He is so rich that He gives me without limit what I ask, although I do not get involved in making up a long catalogue of my wants. As I have two brothers and the novices, the days would not be long enough for me to detail the needs of each soul, and in any case I should be terrified of forgetting something important. Complicated methods are no use to simple souls, and as I am one, Our Lord Himself has given me a very simple little means of fulfilling my obligations.

After Holy Communion one day He made me understand the significance of these words: "Draw me: we will run after Thee to the odor of Thy ointments." So Jesus, there is no need to say: In drawing me, draw also the souls I love. When a soul has been captivated by [God], she cannot run alone. Every soul she loves is drawn after her.

All God's Treasures to Give

—From January 9, 1897 note to Pauline

Dear little Mother, if you only knew how much I was touched when seeing the degree to which you love me! Oh! Never would I be able to show you my gratitude here below. I hope to go soon up above. Since, if there is *a heaven, it is for me*, [and] I shall be rich; I shall have all God's treasures, and He Himself will be my good. Then I shall be able to return to you a hundredfold all I owe you. Oh I am looking forward to it. It troubles me so much to be always receiving without ever giving.

Oh Mother, how beautiful is your lot! It is truly worthy of *you*, the privileged one of our family,* of you who show us the way just as the little swallow that we see always at the head of his companions, tracing out, in the air, the way that must lead them to their new homeland.

---

* Born with a personality that drew others, Agnes of Jesus [Pauline] was the first of the family to become a nun and she had been elected prioress. It was she to whom her dying mother said, "I know you will become a nun—and a saint."

An Unwitting Prophecy
of Her Role After Death

—From her poem "Jesus, my Beloved, Remember!"

This fire from heaven—You have placed it in my soul and I, too, want to spread its passion.

A feeble spark—Oh mystery—suffices to ignite an immense conflagration.

Her Treasure

As a river sweeps along it carries all it meets to the sea. So, my Jesus, the soul plunged into the ocean of Your love carries along its treasures. You know mine are those souls You have linked with mine. As You've entrusted these treasures to me, I dare borrow your words.

[At my life's end] I want to be able to say as You did: "I glorified thee on earth, having accomplished the work which thou gave me to do.... I have manifested thy Name to those thou gavest me.... Holy Father, keep them in thy name ... that they may be one, even as we are one.... Father, I desire that they also, whom thou hast given me may be with me where I am, to behold my glory which thou hast given me in thy love for me before the world's foundation. [May] the love with which thou hast loved me ... be in them, and I in them" (RSV).

Yes, Lord, those are the words I want to repeat before I fly to Your arms. Perhaps presumptuous? No, of course not. For a long time You have let me be bold and free with You [saying] what the prodigal son's father said to his older son: "All that is mine is yours" (RSV). So your words, Jesus, are mine and I can use them to draw the Heavenly Father's favors onto the souls which belong to me.

Wanting Only to Die of Love

How gentle and merciful God is. He sent me this heavy cross [her trial of faith in which it seemed to her that heaven and an afterlife did not exist] just at the time when I was strong enough to bear it. At any other time it would have disheartened me. Now it has only one result: it removes all natural satisfaction from my longing for heaven.

I no longer want anything except to love until I die of love. I am free and fear nothing. I am not even afraid—and it used to be my greatest fear—that my illness will drag out and make me a burden to the community. If it pleases God, I am willing for my suffering, both bodily and spiritual, to last for years. I am not afraid of a long life. I do not refuse the struggle: "The Lord is a rock upon which I stand; He teaches my hands to fight and my fingers to war. He is my protector and I have hoped in Him."

The Way of Divine Intimacy

—From June 21, 1897 letter to Father Belliere

I love [St. Augustine and St. Mary Magdalene] too, their repentance and especially their loving audacity! When I see Magdalene walking up before the many guests, washing with her tears the feet of her adored Master, whom she is touching for the first time, I feel that *her heart* has understood the abysses of love and mercy *of the Heart of Jesus*, and sinner though she is, [He] was not only disposed to pardon her but to lavish on her the blessings of His divine intimacy.

Ever since I have been given the grace to understand also the love of Jesus, it has expelled all fear. The remembrance of my faults humbles me, draws me never to depend on my[self], but speaks to me of mercy and love even more.

Cast[ing] our faults with entire filial confidence into the devouring fire of love, how would these not be consumed?

I know there are some saints who spent their life in astonishing mortifications to expiate their sins, but what of it; "There are many mansions in my Heavenly Father's house," Jesus has said, [so] I follow the way He is tracing out for me and I abandon myself to what Jesus sees fit to do in my soul.

104

Thérèse's Heaven: To Make God Loved by a Multitude

—From July 14, 1897 (the last) letter to Father Roulland

When you receive this letter, no doubt I shall have left this earth. The Lord in His infinite mercy will have opened His kingdom to me, and I shall be able to draw from His treasures in order to grant them liberally to the souls dear to me. Believe, Brother, that your little sister will hold to her promises, and, her soul will joyfully fly toward the distant regions you are evangelizing. Ah! Brother, I feel it—I shall be more useful to you in heaven [so] it is with joy I announce my coming entrance into that blessed city, sure you will thank the Lord for giving me the means of helping you more effectively in your apostolic works.

I really count on not remaining inactive in heaven. My desire is to work still for the Church and for souls. I am asking God for this and I'm certain He will answer me. Are not the angels continually occupied with us without their ever ceasing to see the Divine Face and to lose themselves in the ocean of Love without shores? Why would Jesus not allow me to imitate them?

What attracts me to the homeland of heaven is the Lord's call, the hope of loving Him finally as I have so much desired to love Him, and the thought that I shall be able to make Him loved by a multitude of souls who will bless Him eternally.

Exposed to the Sun of Love

—Process testimony of her sister Marie

Sister Thérèse of the Child Jesus strove all her life to pass unnoticed. She wrote to me on the eve of my profession (1888) "Pray for [me that] I remain always a little grain of sand completely unnoticed, well hidden from every eye, so that Jesus alone can see it, that it becomes more and more tiny until it is reduced to nothing."

She wrote me in 1896: "Ah, if only all weak and imperfect souls felt what the most little of all souls, the soul of your little Thérèse, feels. Not a single one of them would despair of arriving at the summit of the mountain of Love."

Her humility did not keep her from recognizing the privileges that God had given her soul, but she always knew how to credit these to Him. During her illness, on the evening of July 25, 1897, she said to me: "I saw through the window that the setting sun [made] the summit of the trees appear all gold. I said to myself: When one exposes oneself to the sun of Love, then one appears all gold. That's why I appear all gold; I'd cease to be immediately if I drew away from Love."

The Merciful Love of Jesus

—*From July 26, 1897 letter to Father Belliere*

107

I am in total agreement with your opinion: "The Divine Heart is more saddened by the thousand little indelicacies of His friends than by even the grave sins that persons of the world commit"; but it seems to me that it is *only* when His own, unaware of their continual indelicacies, make a habit of them and do not ask His pardon that Jesus [feels thusly]. Regarding those who *love* Him and who come after each indelicacy to ask His pardon by throwing themselves into His arms, Jesus is thrilled with joy. He says to His angels what the father of the prodigal son said to his servants: "Clothe him in his best robe, and place a ring on his finger, and let us rejoice." Ah! how little known are the *goodness*, the *merciful love* of Jesus, Brother! It is true to enjoy these treasures one must humble oneself, recognize one's nothingness, and that is what many souls do not want to do; but, little Brother, this is not the way you act, so the way of simple and loving confidence is really made for you.

On the Blessed in Heaven

—From August 10, 1897 (the last) letter to Father Belliere

108

I admit to you, little Brother, that we do not understand heaven in the same way. It seems to you that sharing in the justice, in the holiness of God [after her approaching death], I would be unable as on earth to excuse your faults. Are you forgetting, then, that I shall be sharing also in the *infinite mercy* of the Lord? I believe the Blessed [that is, all the dead in heaven] have great compassion on our miseries; they remember, being weak and mortal like us, they committed the same faults, sustained the same combats, and their fraternal tenderness becomes greater than it was when they were on earth; and for this reason, they never cease praying for us.

Her Humility at Life's End

109

[Writing of "how small and weak she is" in the third person, Thérèse says]:

Everyone can stoop down over her, admire her, and shower flattery on her, but it won't give her a scrap of that foolish self-satisfaction which would spoil the real happiness she has in knowing that she is nothing but a poor little non-entity in God's eyes. When I say that all praise leaves me unmoved, I'm not thinking of the love and confidence you [Mother Marie de Gonzague, under whose orders she is writing] show me. I'm very moved by it, but I feel that I now need have no fear of praise and that I can accept it calmly. For I attribute to God all the goodness with which He has endowed me. It is nothing to do with me if it pleases Him to make me seem better than I am. He is free to do what He wants.

The Abyss of God's Love

You know, God, that I have never wanted anything but to love You alone. I long for no other glory. Your love has gone before me from my childhood, it has grown with me, and now it is an abyss whose depths I cannot plumb. Love attracts love and mine soars up to You, eager to fill the abyss of Your love, but it is not even a drop of dew lost in the ocean. To love You as You love me, I must borrow Your love—only then can I have peace. O Jesus, it seems to me that You cannot give a soul more love than You have bestowed on me, and that is why I dare ask You to love those You have given me "even as You have loved me." If, one day in heaven, I find out that You love them more than me, I shall rejoice, recognizing that even on earth they must have deserved it more, but meanwhile I cannot imagine any greater love than that You have given me without any merit of my own.

110

She Struts Her Joy

111

I always see the good side of things. There are those [people] who take everything in such a way as to give themselves the most possible distress. For me, it's the opposite. If I have nothing but pure suffering, if heaven is so black that I can't see any light—well, then I make of that my joy. And I strut over it!

Comparing Two Saints

I like Theophane Venard better than St. Louis Gonzaga because the life of St. Louis is extraordinary and his [Blessed Theophane's] is wholly ordinary. Then he speaks of himself, while someone else tells [Gonzaga's] story so one doesn't know hardly anything of his soul.

Theophane Venard loved his family very much; I also love my little family very much. I can't understand the saints who don't love their families.

[Later she continues] At the time when it seemed I'd be departing for [Vietnam], you remember, to have a sign of God's will, [I] began a novena to Theophane Venard. I had returned to full community life, even matins. Well, immediately during the novena I began again to cough, and since then I just get worse and worse. It's he [Venard] who gave me this call [from God]. How I'd love to have his picture; he's a soul who pleases me. St. Louis Gongaza [whose life the nuns were reading at this time] was serious even in recreation, but Theophane Venard, was merry all the time.

A Sense of Humor to the End

113

—Chatting with Pauline in late May 1897

When I get to heaven, how many graces I'll ask for you! Oh I'll torment the good God so much that, even if he wished at first to refuse me, my importuning will force him to crown my desires. That story is in the scriptures....

[Later] If the saints [in heaven] show me less affection than my [four blood] sisters, that will seem truly hard—and I'll go cry in a little corner.

"I Count on Him"

I don't have any fear of the final struggles, nor of sufferings, however great they might be, from my illness [terminal tuberculosis]. The good God has always succored me; He's helped me and led me by the hand from my earliest infancy. I count on Him. I'm certain that He'll continue His [succoring] to the end. I might very well not be able to stand any more but I'll never have too much, I'm sure.

As She Nears Death

—*From June 9, 1897 note to Father Belliere*
I am not dying, I am entering into Life....

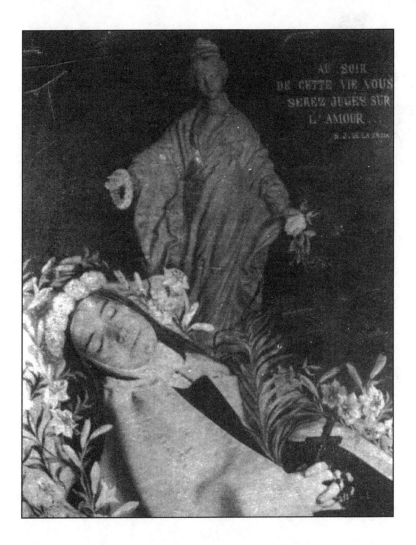

AU SOIR
DE CETTE VIE VOUS
SEREZ JUGÉS SUR
L'AMOUR...

S. J. DE LA CROIX

At Her First Tomb

—Process testimony by Céline

116

The tomb of the Servant of God [Thérèse] has become more and more a place of pilgrimage. Many priests come. After the exhumation of [Thérèse's body] on September 6, 1910, the wooden cross which had been placed over the first grave was carried back to Carmel. This cross was literally covered with inscriptions made by pilgrims expressing their petitions [for Thérèse's prayers to God] and their thanksgivings. The number of pilgrims seems to increase all the time.

On Spiritual Fecundity

Thérèse's youngest cousin, Marie, followed Thérèse into Carmel; Marie's sister, Jeanne, married and—like Thérèse's own mother—dreamed fruitlessly of a priest son. Thérèse prayed mightily for the grace of motherhood for Jeanne, writing in one of her last letters to her aunt and uncle that in heaven she would try to obtain this blessing. But as if intuiting it might not happen, she adds:

"If I am not answered she will be able to rejoice at the thought that in heaven 'The Lord will give her the joy of seeing *herself the mother of many children,'* the souls that her well-accepted sacrifice would bring to birth in the life of grace."

[After Thérèse's death, Jeanne confided to her nun sister in a letter:] "I have seen the truth of [Thérèse's] saying: 'I shall spend my heaven in doing good....' The favors she is granting me are much more precious than if she were to send me the little fair-haired child she promised. She consoles me spiritually; she suggests that I offer up my little sufferings for a priest, and what good this thought has done me! I shall not be able to be the mother of a priest, but I shall be able to bring forth spiritually a servant of God by uniting my sorrows to the merits of Jesus Christ."

A Child's Cure

—A summary of one of many hundreds of favors reported in letters to the Lisieux Carmel

118

A child born April 17, 1903, was only one year old when she became ill with deadly influenza, with such a high fever she went into convulsions. The toddler lived, but was "stone deaf." Mostly she made her wants known by signs.

Her parent had sadly decided to send her to what at the time was called "a deaf and dumb school," where she could hopefully get some sort of education. Then the warmhearted mother of a family the parents were very friendly with learned of their decision. She urged they let her first make a novena to Sister Thérèse of the Child Jesus, begging the child's cure.

A woman of great faith, she did not make this novena quietly. Instead she began the audacious undertaking with the totally deaf little girl kneeling with her for the prayer each day, as if saying, "See this youngster they plan to send away. I've told her you can help. You certainly aren't going to disappoint her now, are you?"

They say God just can't resist people with faith like that—especially when it is expended so unselfishly for someone else. The child remained deaf as a stone on days one, two, and three of the novena, but on the fourth day, the child's mother suddenly noticed her little girl could hear. *[Crowning this healing, Thérèse later appeared to the praying child.]*

At Jesus' Side

In 1915 a young black tradesman in [Dahomey, Africa] [was] studying to become a Christian. Adrien Metamehou Quenum was toting his collection of fetishes—rather uneasily, having been threatened they would take their revenge—to "give them up" to Bishop Francis Steinmetz, [when he] was severely bitten by a normally tame dog. Whether because he was the victim of a shamanistic curse or his body responded to the thought that he was, something like blood poisoning set in and he began to wither away. *[While in a hospital, he was told about Thérèse and began seeking the dead nun's prayers for his cure.]*

August 29th the sick man dreamed he saw Jesus Christ, at whose side was the young saint whose prayers he had begged. Jesus presented her to the sick African, [whom she told], "I'm sent to cure you." She also told Metamehou, "the good God has made me powerful, because, out of love for Him, I knew how to make myself very small."

He woke up filled with joy and perfectly healthy. His entire family—"the very people who had heaped curses on his head when he went to 'turn in' his fetishes"—became Christians too.

An Artist and Writer's Witness

—*Mme. Denise Legrix won the Prix Schweitzer in 1960*

In 1929 I was hospitalized at Caen in a [tuberculosis] sanatorium with several lesions in my left lung. After failed [treatment], considering the gravity of my condition, the doctor offered me a book concerning a young religious of Lisieux who had died of tuberculosis.

"You'll see," he said. "Sister Thérèse is going to cure you."

I accepted with joy and was bowled over. I begged St. Thérèse [for her prayers to God] with all my heart, speaking with a boundless confidence that she heard me.

Because of the failure of the [treatment], I begged Thérèse to [get me out of this place where others were dying].

I dreamed I saw St. Thérèse, holding her crucifix and roses in her arms. I saw a petal from a rose detach and rest on my left side. I woke, weeping, and saying, "Oh Sister Thérèse, thanks, thanks!"

The next morning, my sister arrived and said, "I've come to get you; we've found a treatment you can do at home." *[That same morning the doctor predicted that in three weeks, she'd be dead.]*

Six months later, I had a new X-ray. The stupefied doctor said: "If I hadn't seen the old X-ray, I couldn't believe it's you; there is nothing left but a few scars."

References

<u>DAY</u>

1. *General Correspondence Volume II*, translated by John Clark, O.C.D., (Washington, D.C.: Washington Province of Discalced Friars, Inc., 1988), amended by the editor, 1223-24.
2. Clarke, II, 1231.
3. *General Correspondence, Volume I*, translated by John Clark, O.C.D., (Washington, D.C.: Washington Province of Discalced Friars, Inc., 1982), amended by the editor, 107-8.
4. St. Thérèse of Lisieux, *The Autobiography of St. Thérèse of Lisieux*, translated by John Beevers (New York: Doubleday, 1957), 27.
5. St. Thérèse of Lisieux, 29-31.
6. St. Thérèse of Lisieux, 38-39.
7. St. Thérèse of Lisieux, 55.
8. Process testimony of Soeur Marie-Joseph de la Croix, O.S.B., quoted in *Thérèse de Lisieux* (magazine of the shrine), November 1996, translated by the editor, 7.
9. St. Thérèse of Lisieux, 60.
10. St. Thérèse of Lisieux, 52, modified by the editor.
11. St. Thérèse of Lisieux, 49.
12. St. Thérèse of Lisieux, 57.
13. St. Thérèse of Lisieux, 58.
14. St. Thérèse of Lisieux, 63.
15. St. Thérèse of Lisieux, 66.
16. St. Thérèse of Lisieux, 65, and Stanza One of her poem "My Song for Today," translated by the editor and unknown.
17. St. Thérèse of Lisieux, 66.
18. St. Thérèse of Lisieux, 71.
19. St. Thérèse of Lisieux, 63.
20. Translated by the editor.
21. St. Thérèse of Lisieux, 77-78.
22. St. Thérèse of Lisieux, 81.
23. St. Thérèse of Lisieux, 89.
24. St. Thérèse of Lisieux, 92.
25. St. Thérèse of Lisieux, 98-99.

26. _À Mère Marie de Gonzague_, Deuxieme Partie, translated by the editor, 269-70.
27. Clark, I, 499-500.
28. St. Thérèse of Lisieux, 96-97.
29. St. Thérèse of Lisieux, 148-49.
30. St. Thérèse of Lisieux, 148-49.
31. St. Thérèse of Lisieux, modified by the editor, 156.
32. St. Thérèse of Lisieux, 122.
33. St. Thérèse of Lisieux, 124.
34. _À Mère Marie de Gonzague_, Deuxieme Partie, translated by the editor, 267-68.
35. St. Thérèse of Lisieux, 142.
36. St. Thérèse of Lisieux, modified by the editor, 156.
37. St. Thérèse of Lisieux, modified by the editor, 99.
38. St. Thérèse of Lisieux, 101.
39. St. Thérèse of Lisieux, 103.
40. St. Thérèse of Lisieux, 158.
41. St. Thérèse of Lisieux, 106.
42. From a conversation with her sisters during her final days, translated by John Beevers and quoted in his _St. Thérèse: the Little Flower: the Making of a Saint_, 138.
43. Translated by the editor.
44. Process testimony of Celine reporting Thérèse's words, translated by the editor.
45. St. Thérèse of Lisieux, modified by the editor, 113-14.
46. Clarke, II, 994-95, Beevers translation from _St. Thérèse of Lisieux_, 150.
47. St. Thérèse of Lisieux, 150.
48. St. Thérèse of Lisieux, various translators including the editor, 49. Autobiography, various translators including the editor, 50. Autobiography, Beevers translation modified by the editor, 129-30.
51. Translated by the editor.
52. St. Thérèse of Lisieux, 119-20.
53. St. Thérèse of Lisieux, 132.
54. St. Thérèse of Lisieux, 110-11.
55. St. Thérèse of Lisieux, 159.
56. St. Thérèse of Lisieux, 110-11.
57. St. Thérèse of Lisieux, 98.
58. St. Thérèse of Lisieux, unknown translator.

59. St. Thérèse of Lisieux, 149.
60. St. Thérèse of Lisieux, modified by the editor, 153-55.
61. Clarke, II, 748-49.
62. Clarke, II, modified by the editor, 753.
63. Clarke, II, 778.
64. From Thérèse's conversations with her older sister, Pauline, during the last six months of the saint's life, jotted down by Pauline in what scholars today title the Yellow Notebook and quoted in the French-language _Thérèse de Lisieux_ monthly, December 1996, translated by the editor, 6.
65. From the Notes of Pauline for her Process testimony, 2, quoting Sister Marie of the Eucharist.
66. Clarke, II, 1117.
67. Clarke, I, modified by the editor, 823, and Preparatory Notes for the Bishop's Process.
68. St. Thérèse of Lisieux, 135.
69. From the Yellow Notebook of Pauline, translated by the editor.
70. St. Thérèse of Lisieux, 135.
71. From the Yellow Notebook of Pauline, translated by the editor.
72. Quoted in _Thérèse de Lisieux_, Sept. 1994, translated by the editor, 7.
73. St. Thérèse of Lisieux, modified by the editor, 138.
74. Clarke, II, 801.
75. Clarke, II, 833.
76. Clarke, II, 862.
77. Clarke, II, 862.
78. Clarke, II, 865-66; note #1, 867.
79. Clarke, II, 871.
80. Process testimony given Dec. l, 1910, translated by the editor.
81. Clarke, II, 882.
82. St. Thérèse of Lisieux, 111.
83. Notebook of Sister Marie of the Incarnation, June 6, 1934, 137.
84. St. Thérèse of Lisieux, modified by the editor, 152-53.
85. Quoted in _Thérèse de Lisieux_, Sept. 1994, translated by the editor, 7.
86. St. Thérèse of Lisieux, various translations modified by the editor and the order of some sentences changed to better convey what Thérèse was experiencing.

87. Clarke, II, 951.

88. Clarke, II, 965-66.

89. Thérèse de Lisieux, Sept. 1996, quoting Process testimony given Dec. 2, 1910, translated by the editor.

90. The Yellow Notebook of Pauline, translated by the editor.

91. Clarke, II, 999.

92. Clarke, II, 1014-15.

93. St. Thérèse of Lisieux, 109-10.

94. Clarke, II, 1021.

95. Clarke, II, 1041-42.

96. Notebook of Sister Marie of the Incarnation, July 10, 1934, and Recreation Pieuses number 8, Feb. 8, 1897.

97. Clarke, II, 1093.

98. Clarke, II, 1094.

99. St. Thérèse of Lisieux, 145.

100. Clarke, II, 1046.

101. Stanza 19.

102. St. Thérèse of Lisieux, editor's and other translations.

103. St. Thérèse of Lisieux, 119.

104. Clarke, II, 1133-34.

105. Clarke, II, 1141-42.

106. Translated by the editor.

107. Clarke, II, 1164-65.

108. Clarke, II, 1173.

109. St. Thérèse of Lisieux, modified by the editor, 113.

110. St. Thérèse of Lisieux, 147.

111. From the Yellow Notebook of Pauline quoted in _Thérèse de Lisieux_ magazine, December 1996, translated by the editor, 9.

112. From the Yellow Notebook of Pauline quoted in _Thérèse de Lisieux,_ December 1996, translated by the editor, 7 and 9.

113. From the Yellow Notebook of Pauline quoted in Thérèse de Lisieux, December 1996, translated by the editor, 8.

114. From the Yellow Notebook of Pauline quoted in Thérèse de Lisieux, December, 1996, translated by the editor, 9.

115. Clarke, II, 1128.

116. Translated by the editor.

117. Clarke, II, 1145-47.

118. Archival material from the Lisieux Carmel, excerpted from _Messengers: After-Death Appearances of Saints and Mystics_ by Patricia Treece, 257.

119. Archival material from the Lisieux Carmel excerpted from Messengers: After-Death Appearances of Saints and Mystics by Patricia Treece, 87-89.

120. From Mme. Legrix's testimony in _Thérèse de Lisieux_, April 1994, translated by the editor, 13-14.